Having experienced th[...] th for myself and each of my t[...] has a unique ability to bring ou[...] areas of life. My business, my life, and o[...] and fulfillment have been at an all-time high sin[...] king with her. In this book, Andrea shows you how to get to where you want to be and in no time you will Ignite Your Life!

— KEVIN WILKE, Owner, Nitro Marketing.
www.nitromarketing.com

"I'm always coaching to take action and take it now. Andrea's book is a great resource of concepts and actual action steps you can really use to get moving. Ready go!"

— LORAL LANGEMEIER, CEO/Founder of
Live Out Loud, international speaker,
money expert and best-selling author of
the *Millionaire Maker* 3 book series and
Put More Cash In Your Pocket.
www.liveoutloud.com

Andrea's perspective on living on purpose is a reflection of her unique voice. You'll find her wit, wisdom and unique take on how to get more out of your life in Ignite Your Life! Andrea shares the wisdom of years of coaching on these pages. Listen to her wisdom; apply her suggestions and create the life you love.

— DON OSBORNE, author, coach and trainer.
www.inquarta.com

Ignite Your Life! is a brilliant book about how to create and live a passion filled, purposeful life. It will transform the way you think about how you are living your life and will become your personal GPS System, guiding you True North to Loving the Life that you Live and Living the Life you Love. This book is for anyone who has a desire to live a legendary life, full of Authenticity, Genius and Magic. I invite you to buy as many copies as possible, give them away to the people you love, and watch as the world celebrates the gift that will bless us for generations to come."

— GARRETT LAMBERT, Master NLP Trainer,
Hypnotherapist, Life Strategist Coach.
www.GarrettLambert.com

Begin Loving the Life you Live with the help of this Heartfelt and Inspired work that takes you where most success manuals fail to go. If you haven't been leading the life of your dreams, let Andrea help you leave those limiting beliefs in the dust, get into action and see your new-found passion Ignite Your Life!

— "Juicy" Wees, A Seminar Junkie,
Event Logistics Coordinator.
http://aseminarjunkie.wordpress.com/

Ignite Your Life! is an excellent addition to Andrea's coaching skills. Her humour, vitality and passion are in every page of this book. I'm glad to have read the book, and, more importantly, grateful for the exercises and encouragement inside.

– CONRAD HALL, Author.
www.conradhallcopywriting.com

IGNITE
YOUR LIFE!

How to Get From Where You Are
To Where You Want to Be

ANDREA WOOLF

NEW YORK

IGNITE YOUR LIFE!
How to Get From Where You Are
To Where You Want to Be

by ANDREA WOOLF
© 2010 Andrea Woolf. All rights reserved.

No part of this publication may be reproduced or transmitted in any form or by any means, mechanical or electronic, including photocopying and recording, or by any information storage and retrieval system, without permission in writing from author or publisher (except by a reviewer, who may quote brief passages and/or show brief video clips in a review).

Disclaimer: The Publisher and the Author make no representations or warranties with respect to the accuracy or completeness of the contents of this work and specifically disclaim all warranties, including without limitation warranties of fitness for a particular purpose. No warranty may be created or extended by sales or promotional materials. The advice and strategies contained herein may not be suitable for every situation. This work is sold with the understanding that the Publisher is not engaged in rendering legal, accounting, or other professional services. If professional assistance is required, the services of a competent professional person should be sought. Neither the Publisher nor the Author shall be liable for damages arising herefrom. The fact that an organization or website is referred to in this work as a citation and/or a potential source of further information does not mean that the Author or the Publisher endorses the information the organization or website may provide or recommendations it may make. Further, readers should be aware that internet websites listed in this work may have changed or disappeared between when this work was written and when it is read.

ISBN 978-160037-772-3 (paperback)
Library of Congress Control Number: 2010926118

Published by:

MORGAN JAMES PUBLISHING
1225 Franklin Ave. Ste 325
Garden City, NY 11530-1693
Toll Free 800-485-4943
www.MorganJamesPublishing.com

Cover Design by:
3 Dog Design
www.3dogdesign.net

Interior Design by:
Bonnie Bushman
bbushman@bresnan.net

In an effort to support local communities, raise awareness and funds, Morgan James Publishing donates one percent of all book sales for the life of each book to Habitat for Humanity.
Get involved today, visit
www.HelpHabitatForHumanity.org.

DEDICATION

For my parents,
Leonard and Betty Woolf,
who taught me to follow my heart and my passion.
I love you both and owe you everything.

Ten percent of author proceeds for this book go to Feeding America,
a nonprofit organization dedicated to feeding America's hungry
through a nationwide network of member food banks, as well
as engaging in the fight to end hunger.
I encourage you to join me in supporting this truly
worthwhile cause at www.FeedingAmerica.org.

ACKNOWLEDGMENTS

With my heart brimming with gratitude and appreciation, I would like to acknowledge the following people for their enormous contribution in supporting, sustaining, and challenging me to complete this book:

David Hancock, Rick Frishman, Jim Howard, Bethany Marshall, Margo Toulouse, and the amazing team at Morgan James Publishing for their trust, talent, and compassionate humanity—as well as infinite patience!

My great friend, Don Osborne, for his brilliance and wit, for believing in me, for holding onto my vision even when I wavered, and for empowering me to be and give my best.

My colleague and kindred spirit, master coach Sarah Horton, for her magnificence, great spirit, and powerful leadership.

My amazing and insightful coach, Garrett Lambert, for his passion, commitment, and energy, and for challenging me through the finish line and beyond.

T. Harv Eker and his incredible team of trainers, staff, and volunteers at Peak Potentials Training, for transforming my life, and for showing me the way.

Bob Houle, my colleague and very good friend, who has supported me through the many incarnations of this book, for his powerful insights, for his unconditional support, and mostly for his outrageous and irreverent humor.

My many amazing clients who have taught me so much over the years and encouraged me to put my ideas on paper.

My numerous teachers and mentors along the way who have inspired me to reach for the stars.

Friends and family, too numerous to list, who have supported and encouraged me along the way.

My brother, Paul Woolf, for his support, vast knowledge, expertise, and life experience.

My sister, Jacqueline Woolf, for her brilliance, innate genius, and generosity, and for being the best sister I could have wished for.

My amazing parents, Leonard and Betty Woolf, for being such great parents, always there with their unique wit and wisdom. They continue to teach me so much and shower me daily with their unconditional love and support.

My wonderful husband, Doug Johnson, my partner and adventurer in life, for his belief in me, and his undying patience, love, and support—and for making me laugh when I most needed it.

And lastly, our puppy angels, our two long-haired dachshunds, Fritz and Munchkin, for their endless antics, snuggles, and puppy kisses that never cease to Ignite My Life!

CONTENTS

Part One   Understand The Puzzle Pieces

Part Two   Ignite Your Life!

Part Three   Live An Ignited Life

INTRODUCTION

Every one of us has what it takes to live an ignited life; however, most of us aren't quite experiencing life that way. This book has been written to help you bridge the gap between where you are now and where you want to be. It's intended to be your journey of discovery to uncover what's missing and what it will take for you to truly ignite your life. It gives you a simple system to follow, step by step, to design and live the life of your dreams.

Throughout the writing process, I couldn't help but notice a *glaring poetic irony blinking on and off at me like a bright neon sign*. Here I am, an enlightened, experienced coach, powerfully coaching others to be empowered and in action. "Don't get stopped by anything in your life!" is my advice.

I have been a professional success coach for over fifteen years, coaching all types of people (individuals and business teams) about all kinds of subjects (their businesses or careers, their personal lives, their health, their relationships, fulfillment in life, wanting to make a difference in the world, and so on). It has been a privilege to work with each and every client to help them get clear and _excited_ about every area of their lives.

However, when it came to writing my book, it was a whole other story. At first, I couldn't even bring myself to write a sentence, never mind a paragraph. And a whole book, was I out of my mind?

One of the ways I describe myself is a "recovering perfectionist." That's to say I'm now conscious of my perfectionism, which means that I'm all too aware of when I'm getting in my own way, over-complicating the simple, and generally thinking myself into paralysis. How this showed up in the writing process was insidious, so I really had to keep a close eye on that magnificent mind of mine. When I wasn't paying attention, I would immobilize myself with thoughts like: *"Will I have enough material for the book? What if no one is remotely interested? What if I'm not good enough?"* Does this sound familiar?

Most of us never write the book that we have bursting inside us because we can't sit down and write it word-perfect in one sitting. If I couldn't do that, when would I ever get to it? This was another way my perfectionism reared its ugly head. Notice that this isn't rational. However, it was a wonderfully slippery way of stopping myself from writing. You have to be smart, dare I say brilliant, to complicate things quite so well! Of course it's impossible to sit down and write the complete, perfect, final manuscript, all in one sitting.

Intellectually, I knew that all writing is re-writing. But that didn't stop me from having such crazy thoughts, which, in light of day, make no sense whatsoever. I struggled with doing it perfectly—and over and over again thought and worried myself into paralysis. To get out of my own way, I had to give myself permission to be messy, even incomplete, to just capture the ideas and write them down—then later chunk them down into achievable, manageable pieces to expand and develop. Line by line, and page by page, I did it—I wrote the book.

The very creation of *Ignite Your Life!* has been a cathartic, living incarnation of everything I coach with others. This book is a metaphor for anything in your life you choose to focus on as you move through the chapters. Everything is a work in progress—in other words, everything is a process.

I share this creative angst because this is how most of us way over-complicate and hold ourselves back from reaching for and achieving what we truly want in life. When we step outside what is warm, cozy, and familiar, it feels dark and dangerous out there. This book will help you through your mind chatter, giving you a course to chart through those unknown waters of your mind as you move toward your dreams.

So I say again: every one of us has what it takes to live an ignited life; however, most of us aren't quite experiencing life that way. This book has been written to help you bridge the gap between where you are now and where you want to be. It's intended to be your journey of discovery to uncover what's missing and what it will take for you to truly ignite your life. It will give you a simple system to follow, step by step, to design and live the life of your dreams.

Embrace the fact that right where you are is perfect. Even if it doesn't seem ideal right now, a powerful place to choose as you start this book is in the now, accepting it just the way it is and just the way it isn't. This will create the opening for change and give you power as you make new choices. As you journey through the book, you'll discover that you can cause and create your life to be exactly how you want it to be.

Remember, there is no rule that you have to suffer through any of this process. In fact, most of us achieve far greater results when we're having a great time. So give yourself permission to enjoy each chapter, to savor each process and action step. Breathe and take your time. Dwell on the space between each chapter. Experience it all with freedom and ease. And celebrate the results as you ***Ignite Your Life!***

Love the life you live

Live the life you love

Part One

UNDERSTAND THE PUZZLE PIECES

1

LOVE YOUR LIFE

"Joy is what happens to us when we allow ourselves to recognize how good things really are."

—Marianne Williamson

Imagine what it would be like if you loved absolutely everything about your life. Imagine you aren't holding back at all. Imagine you have no fear and are daring to play bigger than you have ever dared. Imagine a life without resignation, without suffering, without survival or just getting by. Imagine your life is just as you imagine, just the way you want it, and it's totally of your creation.

The skeptics among you may be asking, "What medication is she on?" How could it be possible to say how life will go when there are so many outside influences and circumstances? Most of us have given up being and feeling like we're at the helm of our life. We're overwhelmed with information and activity. We bounce from project to project and react to one person after another. Most of us barely have time to catch our breath, never mind create a life of our own design, the life of our dreams. This is exactly how most of us are living in what we call the "civilized Western world."

And you might be thinking that it's a completely selfish point of view to think only of yourself and your life. So, consider the following: Firstly, there's no rule dictating that creating the life you love is only about you. Surely there are important people in many areas of your life who would be included in that life. Secondly, one of the most common ways that we know we love our life is the degree to which we contribute to others. How can you contribute to others unless you first have some degree of clarity about yourself, who you are, what you stand for, and what lights you up? When you give yourself permission to get clear, especially about what lights you up, you become a beacon of light in the world and a gift to every single person whose life you touch.

Perhaps you've been waiting until "someday when…" to go after your dreams—when circumstances permit, when it's a better time, when you have more time, when the stars are aligned with Neptune, and so on. This is life on hold, treading water, keeping your head just above the waterline—a life of putting things off and, in the process, sucking all the vitality out of them until in your mind they become so unattainable or distant, they sometimes fade and even vanish.

As you've probably guessed by now, this is no way to Ignite Your Life!

The quickest way out of the "putting things off" syndrome is to start right now. Be in the now, and let go of everything that hasn't served you up until now—your limiting beliefs, everything that you're labeling "past failures," in other words, everything that keeps you focused on the past.

By being in the now and accepting yourself right where you are and where you're not, you create the freedom to grow, to change, and to dream. Embrace your "now."

For what reason would you accept anything but an amazing, incredible life? And only _you_ get to say what's amazing and incredible for _you_. Since there is only one "you" in all of your marvelous uniqueness, there's no point in comparing yourself to anyone else—feeling better than or less than others is a waste of time and energy. They aren't you, and you certainly aren't them.

Start to imagine what completely loving your life would look like, feel like, and be like to be living it.

Notice whether you're going to your logical mind and are already trying to figure out how to Ignite Your Life by analyzing the one you have been living. As Albert Einstein so wisely said, "You can't solve a problem with the same level of thinking that created the problem."

You tend to attract and create only that which you can imagine. In other words, whatever you believe is true. Have you noticed that if you don't believe something is possible, it tends to show up that way? In fact, often you will gather empirical data, like a squirrel gathering nuts, to prove that you were right. So, if you want to attract more, then you need to expand you and your imagination—in other words, what you believe is possible, especially for yourself.

It's time for you to begin the journey toward living the life you love, and loving the life you live.

Action Steps:

We're going to go through some questions to help you identify role models.

- Who do you know who loves their life? Make a list of people you think enjoy their life:

  _____

  _____

  _____

  _____

  _____

- Who do you know who has no limits and no self-inflicted boundaries? Make a list of people who you see as unlimited and possibility thinkers:

  _____

  _____

  _____

  _____

  _____

- Who do you know who has done amazing things with their life, no matter what circumstances or life events happened? Make a list of people who have overcome and achieved in their life:

_____

_____

_____

_____

_____

BE THE BEST YOU

"The whole point of being alive is to evolve into the complete person you were intended to be."

—Oprah Winfrey

Since you're the source of everything in your life, let's explore this idea of being the best you. When you show up playing and giving 100 percent, that's when you're likely to be the proudest of yourself and be leading a happy, ignited life. Let's take a look at your relationship with yourself, how you see yourself, and how you treat yourself.

ROLES

Think of the many roles that you play and the various hats that you wear. Here are some examples:

- Husband or wife
- Boyfriend or girlfriend
- Father or mother
- Grandfather or grandmother

- Brother or sister
- Son or daughter
- Uncle or aunt
- Cousin
- Extended family member
- Godparent
- Contributor
- Innovator
- Business owner
- Boss
- Manager
- Team leader
- Employee
- Provider
- Homemaker
- Friend
- Teacher
- Student
- Coach
- Coachee
- Motivator
- Mentor
- Caregiver
- Volunteer

How do you show up in each of your roles? Are you being and giving your best? How could you be doing more to be the best _____ (boss, parent, caregiver, etc.)?

SELF-IMAGE

What is your self-image? How do you see yourself? Is it what your parents told you about yourself? Or your family, friends, or colleagues?

Are you happy with how you see yourself? Are you satisfied with every aspect? Or are there some areas you would like to improve? If so, what are those areas, and what specifically would you like to improve?

Do you love yourself? Do you accept yourself just the way you are and just the way you aren't? Or are you hard on yourself?

How do you see and treat yourself?

PHYSICAL

If you're like most people, you're leading a very busy life. One of the key areas that's often overlooked and suffers is physical health. It's all too easy to be too busy, to not have the time, to be too tired to not take care of your health. However, the irony is that this needs to come first, in order to create the energy to be able to handle everything else.

How important do you make physical health in your life, on a scale of 0–10 (0 = low, 10 = high)?

How would you describe your physical health? Is it excellent, couldn't be better? Or is there room for improvement? If so, how?

How would you describe how you take care of yourself? This could include exercise and nutrition, as well as other factors, from getting enough rest to being good to yourself.

What could you be doing to improve your physical health?

EMOTIONAL

Emotions play a very important role in our overall well-being. The pathway to optimal health is creating balance between our physical body and our emotional state.

What stress do you have in your life? Within your family, at work? What about when your car or your computer isn't working properly? How do you handle stress? What do you do to reduce and release it?

Here are some ideas:

- Talk to a friend
- Meditate
- Practice yoga
- Sleep eight hours a night
- Use hypnosis
- Eat healthy
- Listen to calming music

One way of defining emotional health is the ability to express all emotions appropriately. In other words, you're clear about your emotions and are able to be authentic (true to yourself) and express yourself fully and appropriately.

Where in your life aren't you clear about how you feel? Where are you not fully expressed? And how could you express yourself appropriately—in other words, so that there is the highest outcome possible for all concerned? This is **_not_** to create extreme upset, get fired, or just plain be right in the matter!

SPIRITUAL

In the day-to-day business of life, it's all too easy to overlook the spiritual area. For some people, this means religious practice. If, for you, being the best you in this area is committing to going to your church, synagogue, or mosque regularly and on major holidays, and then doing so, so be it.

For others, your spirituality might be expressed more in the metaphysical realm—by going within through meditation, seeking that which connects all of us to one another in order to find deeper meaning.

Perhaps you're called to express your spirit by getting more involved in your community through outreach into the community and beyond, doing good work.

A healthy spirit means so many different things to different people. From a broader perspective, it's a sense of wholeness, a sense of knowingness, a sense of something far greater than what we can see and touch.

How do you live and express your spirituality?

Are you happy with where it is, or would you like it to be deeper? If so, what would that look like?

CELEBRATING LIFE

It's impossible to be the best you and not be having any fun. It's imperative to enjoy life to the fullest and to look for every opportunity to celebrate in order to truly be the best you. It's a hollow victory to be a superstar in your business or career, to be in top physical condition and in great health, to have great relationships, and to feel great about yourself, and yet not enjoy your life.

It's all about enjoying the journey, not just the destination. In what we call the "civilized Western world," we often race from one project or achievement to the next, barely catching our breath before we scurry on to the next one. It's vital to give yourself pause to celebrate the moments and then move on.

Be outrageous! Have fun "just because." It's not necessarily about how much time you take to celebrate. This can be done in moments if you say so. Sometimes just stepping away from your desk for five or ten minutes to go outside and take in the sunshine and blue sky or whatever is around you can transform your day. Taking a moment to share a tender kiss with your loved one brings a spring to your step. And pausing to hug your children and tell them how much you love them touches everyone's heart and changes all of you forever.

How much are you enjoying your life?

Where in your life is there room for more fun and celebration?

What could you celebrate today?

MAKING A DIFFERENCE

We often have the most significant experiences of being our best when we're contributing to other people, giving of our time and/or money to a great cause, a person, or a group in need. You almost always get so much more than you give. It's a fine thing to achieve more in life, to earn more, to acquire more stuff. However, for most of us, how we really get to feel proud of ourselves is when we experience this thing called 'making a difference in the world.'

How are you making a difference in your community and in the world?

How do you feel about it?

Also, notice how you're designing your life. Is it alone or do you have team around you? Are you usually a loner or a team player? If you're a loner, you might want to try letting others support you as a team. With others you'll see that the results are exponential. As T. Harv Eker so insightfully says, "How you do anything is how you do everything."

Are you really involved, moderately so, or barely?

There are no right or wrong, good or bad answers, only the opportunity to observe how you take on making a difference in the world.

Could you be doing more?

That could mean giving more time and effort. It could also mean finding ways to make the time you're already contributing more valuable.

Could you be giving more of yourself?

For almost twenty years, I was involved in many projects to help the homeless in Los Angeles. One of those was an on-going program to provide food to hundreds and hundreds on a regular basis. All of the volunteers did a marvelous job setting up and serving the food. Their commitment and dedication were dazzling and unquestionable. However, many could not look the people they were serving in the eye, and few of the volunteers knew the people they were serving by name, even though most of them came back week after week.

This is not to judge—just to present the idea that there's always an opportunity if you're looking for it to learn more about yourself, what motivates you, and what holds you back. For example:

- obligation
- all the "shoulds" in your life
- looking good
- status
- visibility
- recognition
- peer pressure
- expectation of something in return
- unconditional giving
- love
- passion
- caring

This is the opportunity for you to look at where you are. Wherever that is, you're well on your way to being the best you. It's all about the journey, not just the destination, and we're all somewhere along our journey in each of these areas.

Action Steps:

Now it's for you to decide where you want to make some changes.

- What do you love about yourself? What don't you love about yourself? What do you want to change? Make a list of your answers:

I love:	I don't love:	I want to change:
_____	_____	_____
_____	_____	_____
_____	_____	_____
_____	_____	_____
_____	_____	_____

- What do others love about you? What don't others love about you? What do you want to change? Write down your answers.

Others love:	Others don't love:	I want to change:
_____	_____	_____
_____	_____	_____
_____	_____	_____
_____	_____	_____

_____ _____ _____

_____ _____ _____

- Check off areas where you want to make changes:
    - ◆ Roles
    - ◆ Self-Image
    - ◆ Physical
    - ◆ Emotional
    - ◆ Spiritual
    - ◆ Celebrating Life
    - ◆ Making a Difference
    - ◆ Other: _____

ACCEPT YOURSELF

"Have the daring to accept yourself as a bundle of possibilities and undertake the game of making the most of your best."

—Harry Emerson Fosdick

To create any change in your life, it starts with awareness.

There's no such thing as a problem. Everything is circumstance, unless we get out our label maker, print out a label, and stick it on as if it's real and permanent. Everything is an opportunity. And there are two basic ways to react: to resist it and fight it, or to accept it so that you can move forward.

Non-acceptance of self is victimhood. You are a victim of yourself, your own judgment of yourself. Most of us are harder on ourselves than anybody else and, through our own internal dialogue (which is usually less than inspiring), we talk ourselves into victimhood.

The resistance is the problem. And resistance is equal to suffering. And as most of us know only too well, "what we resist persists."

In order to move from here to anywhere, it starts with getting clear about where you are and accepting it—being at peace with it and embracing it versus judging it, wishing it were different, and beating yourself up about it. Accept what you don't accept about yourself.

Everything is an opportunity if you say so.

It's the emotion that we attach to things that keeps us stuck. Repeated emotions turn into beliefs. For example, you're beating yourself up because of the extra weight you're carrying and that voice inside your head is saying over and over again, "I'll never be thin."

Everything that we have and everything that we are in our lives is ultimately about creation. On some level, we have played a role in it being the way it is. So wherever you have emotion around an area in your life—for example, frustration—take a look at what you have either done or not done to contribute to it. This is how you ultimately achieve acceptance and take your power back.

So, let's say you're frustrated about your weight or the way you look. Changing it first starts with accepting yourself right where you are, embracing every extra ounce that you're carrying since you had something to do with it being there! From this place of acceptance, you will now be able to free yourself up from paralysis (both emotional and physical) and start to build a plan around how you will release whatever the desired amount is to get to your ideal weight. You will find the journey so much easier and more enjoyable if you embrace yourself and bring yourself along for the ride.

The four steps to self-acceptance are:

1. Become aware

2. Accept what is

3. Create a plan

4. Stay open

Action Steps:

- Pick the top area in your life where you're not happy and content. Write down what it is and, in 20 words or less, describe how you feel about it.

_____

_____

_____

_____

_____

- What have you done that has contributed to it? Or what have you not done or avoided doing that has contributed to it?

_____

_____

_____

_____

_____

- What will it take to accept yourself right where you are? Write down your answer.

_____

_____

_____

_____

_____

- What three action steps will you take right now? Write down your answer.

1. _____

2. _____

3. _____

HOW DO YOU GET
YOURSELF STUCK?

"Most of the barriers to your success are man-made. And most often, you're the man who made them."

—Frank Tiger

You're probably reading this book because you're stuck somewhere in your life! The very fact that you made the effort to seek out this book, choose it, and invest in it speaks volumes about who you are: you're yearning to do something about it, committed to growing and learning, taking on new approaches, and definitely wanting to achieve in your life.

You're also probably extremely smart. As a coach, I naturally attract super-smart people. So, by the Law of Attraction, the odds are high that you're extremely smart. On the one hand, there's a huge amount to acknowledge: your knowledge, your experience, and your accomplishments—that's everything you already know and have already done. On the other hand, there's the flip side of that very same coin. When you're so smart, when you have so much knowledge, experience and so many accomplishments, you can do a great job of getting yourself mightily stuck—for example, talking yourself in and out of taking action, thinking yourself into paralysis, and overwhelming yourself with everything that might go wrong.

Notice what barriers you have erected that are getting in the way of achieving success. By taking a powerful inventory of ways that you're getting in your own way, you can identify how to deal with them, get around them, and eliminate them, then accelerate your journey toward success.

As we get to the list of just *some* of the ways that you get yourself stuck, keep these two tips in mind:

1. Remember, you have to be extremely smart to come up with them!

2. Remember to keep breathing!

WAYS TO GET YOURSELF STUCK

As you read through the list, put an 'x' against each one that makes you go "OUCH" and put an 'x' against each one that makes you "GIGGLE."

Ouch	Giggle	Ways to Get Yourself Stuck
❏	❏	Lack of planning
❏	❏	Lack of organization
❏	❏	Lack of a system and process
❏	❏	Having no direction
❏	❏	Having no destination

HOW DO YOU GET YOURSELF STUCK?

❏	❏	Having no vision
❏	❏	Having no plan
❏	❏	Having no goals
❏	❏	Relying on memory
❏	❏	Keeping everything in your head
❏	❏	Not writing everything down
❏	❏	All talk and no action
❏	❏	Preparing to prepare
❏	❏	Planning to plan
❏	❏	Meeting about meetings
❏	❏	Not prioritizing
❏	❏	Taking care of everyone else
❏	❏	Taking care of everything except the most important and/or urgent
❏	❏	Over-committing
❏	❏	Multi-tasking
❏	❏	Doing too many things at the same time
❏	❏	Taking on too many projects
❏	❏	Taking on too much at one time
❏	❏	Getting distracted (by people, e-mail, telephones, etc.)
❏	❏	Not making it important enough
❏	❏	Setting unrealistic timelines and deadlines

❏	❏	Underestimating how long everything will take
❏	❏	Over-scheduling
❏	❏	Not scheduling everything
❏	❏	Not scheduling anything
❏	❏	Being too smart
❏	❏	Saying "I know that"
❏	❏	Knowing how it is
❏	❏	Not knowing what to do, how to do it, etc.
❏	❏	Yes but…
❏	❏	That won't work because…
❏	❏	I can't because…
❏	❏	Nobody can do it as well as I can
❏	❏	Being hard on yourself
❏	❏	Over-thinking
❏	❏	Over-complicating
❏	❏	Being a perfectionist
❏	❏	Needing it to be perfect or not done at all
❏	❏	Needing to be right
❏	❏	Fear of being wrong
❏	❏	Having an attachment to the outcome
❏	❏	Not asking for help

HOW DO YOU GET YOURSELF STUCK?

❑	❑	By the time I explain it to someone else I could do it myself
❑	❑	It's quicker to do it myself
❑	❑	Needing to do it all at once or not at all
❑	❑	Going it alone
❑	❑	Being strong
❑	❑	Being independent
❑	❑	Isolating yourself
❑	❑	Not believing in yourself
❑	❑	Believing it's impossible
❑	❑	Believing it will never work
❑	❑	Negative self-talk
❑	❑	Negative thinking—I can't
❑	❑	Limiting beliefs—I'm too dumb; I'm too short; I'm unlucky in love
❑	❑	Listening to too many people
❑	❑	Having trouble saying no
❑	❑	Worrying about what others will think or say
❑	❑	Talking yourself in and out of it
❑	❑	Allowing yourself to be stopped by criticism
❑	❑	Not asking for feedback
❑	❑	Getting too many opinions

❑	❑	Listening to criticism
❑	❑	Listening to others
❑	❑	Not listening to others
❑	❑	Listening to the limiting beliefs of others
❑	❑	Avoiding
❑	❑	Delaying
❑	❑	Procrastinating
❑	❑	Putting it off
❑	❑	Paralysis
❑	❑	Being a victim
❑	❑	Blaming everything and everyone else
❑	❑	Impatience
❑	❑	Putting yourself second
❑	❑	Getting emotional (upset, angry, frustrated)
❑	❑	Getting overwhelmed
❑	❑	Focusing on the problem vs. the solution
❑	❑	Imagining the worst
❑	❑	Expecting the worst
❑	❑	Not taking a risk
❑	❑	Coping
❑	❑	Suffering

HOW DO YOU GET YOURSELF STUCK?

❑	❑	Settling
❑	❑	Surviving
❑	❑	Resignation
❑	❑	Losing focus
❑	❑	Losing courage
❑	❑	Giving up
❑	❑	Lack of commitment
❑	❑	Lack of clarity
❑	❑	Lack of focus
❑	❑	Lack of follow-through
❑	❑	Lack of consistency
❑	❑	Lack of stick-to-itiveness
❑	❑	Starting and not completing
❑	❑	Not "chunking it down" to bite-size, manageable pieces
❑	❑	Going in a million directions at once
❑	❑	Having to do it all now
❑	❑	Fear
❑	❑	Fear of rocking the boat
❑	❑	Fear of upsetting others
❑	❑	Fear of rejection
❑	❑	Fear of failure
❑	❑	Fear of not doing it right
❑	❑	Fear of not doing it perfectly
❑	❑	Fear of looking silly or stupid

❏	❏	Fear of not looking good
❏	❏	Fear of standing out
❏	❏	Fear of not making it
❏	❏	Fear of not being good enough
❏	❏	Fear of success
❏	❏	Having no balance in life
❏	❏	Not getting enough sleep or rest
❏	❏	Not getting enough exercise
❏	❏	Not taking care of yourself
❏	❏	Not paying attention to your health
❏	❏	Not having a moment to spare
❏	❏	No contingency time
❏	❏	No margin of time or energy
❏	❏	No reserves
❏	❏	Not staying focused on the present and the future
❏	❏	Holding onto hurt
❏	❏	Dwelling on past failure
❏	❏	Living in the past
❏	❏	Playing it safe
❏	❏	Staying under the radar—maybe they won't notice
❏	❏	Playing "what if…it doesn't work/fit/ start/get off the ground, etc.?"
❏	❏	Holding back

HOW DO YOU GET YOURSELF STUCK?

❏	❏	Playing small
❏	❏	Trying to please everybody
❏	❏	Losing sight of your dream
❏	❏	Losing your passion
❏	❏	Worrying
❏	❏	Doubt
❏	❏	Complaining
❏	❏	Blaming
❏	❏	Losing focus
❏	❏	Explaining, justifying, and defending
❏	❏	Comparing yourself to others
❏	❏	Feeling less than others
❏	❏	Overreacting
❏	❏	Making mountains out of molehills
❏	❏	Not managing yourself
❏	❏	Moving too fast
❏	❏	Moving too slowly
❏	❏	Waiting until you feel like it
❏	❏	Waiting until the perfect moment
❏	❏	Waiting to get motivated and inspired
❏	❏	Waiting until the moon is aligned with Neptune
❏	❏	Wishful thinking

Action Steps:

- Look at the ways *you* get *yourself* stuck. Write down your top ten OUCHES and your top ten GIGGLES. Use the above list and feel free to add your own.

My Top 10 OUCHES

1. _____
2. _____
3. _____
4. _____
5. _____
6. _____
7. _____
8. _____
9. _____
10. _____

My Top 10 GIGGLES

1. _____
2. _____
3. _____
4. _____
5. _____
6. _____
7. _____
8. _____
9. _____
10. _____

- Now we're going to prioritize what makes you wince or giggle the most. Put your list in order, with your biggest OUCH and GIGGLE in the No. 1 spot.

HOW DO YOU GET YOURSELF STUCK?

My Top 10 OUCHES

1. _____
2. _____
3. _____
4. _____
5. _____
6. _____
7. _____
8. _____
9. _____
10. _____

My Top 10 GIGGLES

1. _____
2. _____
3. _____
4. _____
5. _____
6. _____
7. _____
8. _____
9. _____
10. _____

- Write down the top 3 from each of those lists so we can focus on those.

My Top 3 OUCHES

1. _____
2. _____
3. _____

My Top 3 GIGGLES

1. _____
2. _____
3. _____

- For each OUCH and GIGGLE, answer the following questions:

  What one thing do you need to do differently right now to get unstuck?

  For example, if one of your choices is to do with over-scheduling, what will it take to change it? What are you willing to do differently, say no to, schedule differently?

OUCH 1	_____	GIGGLE 1	_____
OUCH 2	_____	GIGGLE 2	_____
OUCH 3	_____	GIGGLE 3	_____

  What do you need to change about yourself today to get unstuck?

  If you select "waiting until you feel like it," what will it take to push through that and do it now?

  If it's "getting distracted," what are you getting distracted by? What will it take to manage that distraction?

OUCH 1	_____	GIGGLE 1	_____
OUCH 2	_____	GIGGLE 2	_____
OUCH 3	_____	GIGGLE 3	_____

YOUR LIFE
BALANCE PUZZLE

"Be aware of wonder. Live a balanced life—learn some and think some and draw and paint and sing and dance and play and work every day some."

—Robert Fulghum

Imagine that your life is like a jigsaw puzzle, made up of key elements. These include:

- Business/Career
- Money
- Romance
- Family
- Friends
- Home
- Fun and Leisure
- Health and Well-Being
- Personal Growth (Spirituality / Learning)

- Gifting Time and/or Money (Making a Difference / Community)

Let's clarify each area.

BUSINESS/CAREER

This is what you do in the world, either through your own business or your job. This is how you fill your working hours. This is how you answer that so-often-asked question: "What do you do?"

MONEY

This is how you feel about how you're doing in this area of your life. It's not about how much money, real estate, or investments you have. To illustrate this, there are multi-millionaires walking the planet who will never have enough, will never feel content, and conversely, there are people on minimum wage who are completely fulfilled.

ROMANCE

This is that special relationship in your life—the relationship with your significant other, your life partner, or your spouse. This is the area of your life where you express, share, and experience love with someone special.

FAMILY

This is the group of people either you were born into or you acquired along the way by one means or another. They are often the ones you are closest to and who are at times the most crazy-making. They may know you only too well, or maybe think they do. They can offer the greatest opportunity to learn, and then you choose to be either like them or exactly the opposite!

FRIENDS

These are the people you choose to share your life with, either on a light, casual, social level or on a deeper, perhaps longer-term level. For some, these may be the people you play with; for others, they are the ones you know you can count on at any time. You may have tons of friends, or you may be able to count your friends on one hand.

HOME

This is the place where you live—whether you own, rent, or share it, this is where you call home. It's the roof over your head, your battlefield or your refuge, as the case may be.

FUN AND LEISURE

This is anything you deem fun and relaxing—from skydiving to meditating, from getting together with great friends to taking a wonderful nap. For those who are completely driven, you may have forgotten what fun is and how to relax. Don't worry, it's like riding a bicycle—it will quickly come back to you!

HEALTH AND WELL-BEING

This is the area of your physical health. This might also include how you take care of yourself in various ways—for example, exercise, diet and nutrition, rest, etc.

PERSONAL GROWTH
(SPIRITUALITY / LEARNING)

This means different things to different people. For some, learning can come from life experience. For others, it is more in the area of spirituality. It can mean growing through seminars or reading. And it can also include working with a coach!

GIFTING TIME AND/OR MONEY
(MAKING A DIFFERENCE / COMMUNITY)

This is the altruistic, gifting area of your life. This is how you choose to make a difference in the world. It can be about gifting money by donating to your favorite charity. Or it can be about gifting your time by volunteering. And it can also be about creating an organization and enrolling the support of others in their gifting of time and/or money. This could also include how you feel about your level of involvement with your immediate, local, national, and/or world community.

As you read this, you're probably experiencing more success in certain areas of your life than others. You are most likely happier with the progress you're making in certain areas of your life and would like things to be very different in other areas.

Let's start by taking a look at how you feel about your life. Is it calm and serene, with every area in perfect balance? How often do you experience it as overwhelmingly busy as you bounce from one thing to the next? There's so much to do, so many people to take care of, you can barely catch your breath and never have enough time for it all. You find yourself almost in survival mode, reacting to whatever presents itself as the most urgent, and race from one project or person to the next. Does this sound familiar?

Before you get overwhelmed and paralyzed with the potential magnitude of it all, let's break it down into the key areas in your life—your **Life Balance Puzzle**. As you read this, refer to the **Life Balance Puzzle** graphic on **Page 48** and go to www.IgniteYourLifeBook.com for your free PDF version to download and print out.

YOUR LIFE BALANCE PUZZLE:

In your **Life Balance Puzzle**, you'll see that there are ten key areas in your life, each with ten puzzle pieces.

Focus on each area one at a time. Take a moment and think about how you feel about each area in the present moment—not how you wish it had been ten years ago, last month, or last week, nor what you hope it's going to be ten days, ten weeks, or ten years from now, just in the present moment.

Remember, there are no right or wrong, good or bad, or "perfect" answers about how you feel about the various areas of your life. How you rate each area merely reflects how you feel right now. It's just a number, and if you so choose, it will create an opportunity for you to cause change in your life. Imagine what your life will be like then…!

Focus on how you feel about each area. For example, in the area of Money, remember it's not about how much money, real estate, or investments you have. It's about how you feel about where you are right now in this area.

Be honest. This is your tool to get clarity about where you are, where you're stuck, and where you would like to get to. There is no one to impress. This is between you and yourself. The more honest you are about how you feel about each area in your life in the present moment, the quicker you'll discover how to get to where you want to be.

Keep your top 3 OUCHES and your top 3 GIGGLES in mind. You already know what they are and what you need to do differently and change. So use them to easily create your **Life Balance Puzzle**.

Take the **Life Balance Puzzle** on like a game. Enjoy the process! Let go of feeling bad and regretting what you haven't done in the past. If you're still reading, you're clearly up to the challenge of achieving in your life, building on where you already are, and reaching new levels of achievement and fulfillment.

Action Steps:

- Rate each area in your **Life Balance Puzzle** on a scale of 1–10, 1 being lowest (couldn't be worse) and 10 being highest (couldn't be better). Circle the number that applies to you.

    - Remember not to judge how you feel about the number that you give each area. It's just a number, and it gives you clarity about where you're at right now. This is just a benchmark.

YOUR LIFE BALANCE PUZZLE

Business/Career	1	2	3	4	5	6	7	8	9	10
Money	1	2	3	4	5	6	7	8	9	10
Romance	1	2	3	4	5	6	7	8	9	10
Family	1	2	3	4	5	6	7	8	9	10
Friends	1	2	3	4	5	6	7	8	9	10
Home	1	2	3	4	5	6	7	8	9	10
Fun and Leisure	1	2	3	4	5	6	7	8	9	10
Health and Well-Being	1	2	3	4	5	6	7	8	9	10
Personal Growth	1	2	3	4	5	6	7	8	9	10
Gifting time and/or Money	1	2	3	4	5	6	7	8	9	10

IGNITE YOUR LIFE!

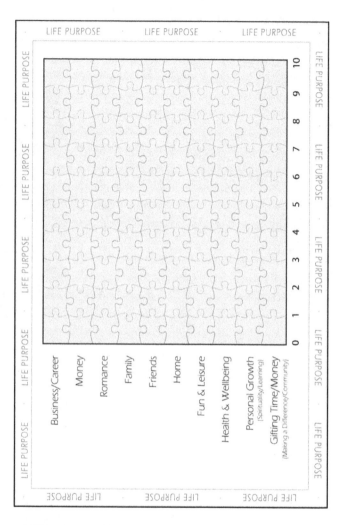

- Fill in the puzzle pieces.

- For example, if you rated your Business as 5, fill in 5 puzzle pieces. If you rated your Health as 7, fill in 7 puzzle pieces, and so on. Make it fun by using colored pens, colored pencils, or crayons!

WHERE ARE YOU STUCK?

"At first our dreams seem impossible, then they seem improbable, but when we summon the will, they become inevitable."

—Christopher Reeve

Looking at your **Life Balance Puzzle**, how did you rate all the areas in your life? Did you give them all a 10? Probably not! Most of us have different things going on in our lives at any moment in time and, hence, feel differently about each area as we balance and re-balance our busy lives.

Have you noticed that your life is a little out of balance?

Congratulations! You're human!

Most of us are out of balance somewhere in our lives.

For now, let's start by selecting one area in your life to focus on first. I strongly suggest that you stay with that area as you move through the processes in this book, so that you don't get overwhelmed and paralyzed, and then put the book aside. You can always come back at a later date and use these processes for every area in your life.

Here are some questions to help you clarify which area you will pick:

- In which area are you the most stuck?
- Where is there an opportunity for your life to be clearer or more effective?
- Which area of your life would you like to change the most or first?
- Where could you be more ignited in your life?

Refer back to your top 3 OUCHES and your top 3 GIGGLES.

- To help you clarify even more specifically:
- Do you love your business every day?
- Are you completely fulfilled in your career?
- Would you rather be doing something else? If so, what?
- Are you ecstatic with where you are financially?
- Would you like your financial picture to be different?
- How is your relationship going with your significant other? Is it just okay? Could it be more amazing and passionate?
- Do you yearn to be in a relationship?
- How are your relationships with your family members? Could they be closer/warmer/more connected?
- What are your relationships with your friends like? Would you like them to be deeper?

- Would you like to have more friends? Or different friends?

- Is your home everything that you ever dreamed it would be?

- How would you like your home to be different?

- Are you having more fun than you can stand in your life?

- Could you be enjoying your life more?

- Have you been taking good care of yourself?

- Have you been putting off taking care of yourself, eating healthier, and exercising?

- Are you tired of feeling tired?

- What would you take on learning if you just had the time and/or money?

- How would you like to grow if you just had the time?

- Are you delighted with how you make a difference in the world by giving of your time and/or money?

- Would you like to make more of a difference in the world?

Action Steps:

- Select one area from your **Life Balance Puzzle** where you want to be more ignited in your life, an area where you want to achieve greater results. Write it down.

Part Two

IGNITE YOUR LIFE!

START WITH THE
BIG PICTURE

"What one thing would you dare to dream if you knew you could not fail?"

—Brian Tracy

Now that you've completed your **Life Balance Puzzle** and chosen which area in your life you want to transform, it's important to create clear vision before leaping into action like a greyhound.

Have you ever been excited about taking something on in your life and scurried into action, only to see your energy and focus fizzle within a few days? And then life starts to happen and gets in the way?

Here are the reasons it's absolutely essential to create clear and powerful vision:

- To create the clear picture of the future for you to live into and move toward

- To have the end clearly in mind
- To inspire you
- To keep you going through whatever it takes to fulfill your vision
- To measure your progress against it
- To light the way

So now let's start with the big picture and create your ideal vision in the area of your life you have chosen.

Imagine you had rated that area a 10, what would be different? What is the gap from where you are to a 10? What's missing in order for that area of your life to be a 10? What would have it be so amazing, so ideal, so great that it merited a 10? Write down all your thoughts, either as a checklist or stream-of-consciousness notes or full sentences. There's no one perfect way to do this. Choose the way that's the easiest and gives you access to your creativity. The idea is to capture all of your ideas—so no editing!

As you go through this creative process, give yourself permission to be dazzled by your own courage and by the vision you've chosen for yourself. Notice how big you're allowing yourself to play. If your tummy isn't tingling, you're probably playing it safe. Allow yourself to dream and dream big. You're creating your future, so make it exciting!

Write it all down. No matter how big your vision is, how many items it includes, write it all down. At this stage, capture the topics. Create headings for each one and then move on. We'll come back to figuring out what it will take to achieve it later.

NOTE: This is where most of us get supremely stuck. If we can't figure it all out immediately, we get overwhelmed and paralyzed, then give up. Just write down the key elements of your vision and fill in the details later.

Give up the idea that it's going to be perfect the first time you put pen to paper or fingers to the keyboard—there's no such thing as the perfect first draft. Watch out for the strong urge to keep editing in order to make it perfect and/or to scrap it completely because of negative self-talk—for example, it will never work; I'll never be able to achieve it; who am I kidding?; etc. Give yourself creative freedom to capture all the brilliant ideas you have for the coming months or years. Let go of judgment and limited thinking and write it all down.

Be wonderfully messy and disorganized. Know that you will be playing with your vision later—to expand it, organize it, edit it, and prioritize it. For those perfectionists among you, it will all be okay. Go ahead, be messy. Just keep writing.

Then have the courage to stick to your dreams. Keep reminders all around you, in words, pictures, and whatever keeps your dreams alive. Napoleon Hill expressed this so powerfully when he said, "Cherish your visions and your dreams as they are the children of your soul, the blueprints of your ultimate accomplishments."

BE SPECIFIC—WHAT AND BY WHEN

Here's an important key: know your desired outcome and write it down in the present tense, as if you have already achieved it and are already there. To get you to being specific, it's okay to start with a general statement. For example:

- I am in the perfect supportive, loving relationship.

- My book is a *New York Times* best-seller.

- My business is a huge success—double the sales and I have more free time.

- I am in excellent health, strong in body, mind, and spirit.

Whatever you're taking on in your life, it's vital to know what you want to achieve and where you want to arrive before starting out.

And now add "by when." You need to know where you're heading so you'll know when you get there, and then celebrate!

Visualize yourself having already accomplished your vision, as if you're already "there." Revel in every detail. Use all your senses. What do you feel, see, hear, and smell? Contemplate what it took to get you there. See, feel, and experience it in every way. Be "WOWED" by it. Write everything down. This is your road map.

Start **now**! Don't put it off as you've probably been doing for a while, and then look back a year from now and regret not having done anything.

And most important of all, give yourself permission to be excited by your own vision. If you're not excited by it, expand your vision until you are!

Action Steps:

- Write down your vision in the present tense.

_____

_____

_____

_____

_____

_____

_____

_____

- Add "by when" to each item in your vision. Be as specific as possible with the timeframe and the date.

_____

_____

_____

_____

_____

_____

_____

_____

_____

_____

- Check how excited you are. Expand your vision until your tummy tingles with excitement! What comes to mind?

_____

_____

_____

_____

_____

_____

_____

_____

_____

8

LIVE YOUR VALUES

"As you live your values, your sense of identity, integrity, control, and inner-directedness will infuse you with both exhilaration and peace. You will define yourself from within rather than by people's opinions or by comparisons to others."

—Stephen R. Covey

Often, despite success and achievement, it's not uncommon to yearn for a greater sense of fulfillment and happiness. Does your life sometimes feel empty? Do you yearn for it to feel full but don't know where to begin? Does it sometimes feel like you have one foot on the brake and one foot on the accelerator, like you're stopping and starting over and over again?

In the scurry of life, have you lost touch with what matters most to you? Have you lost your focus? Are you living your life way out of alignment with how you would like to be living it?

The following is the list of the key areas in your life from your **Life Balance Puzzle**:

- Business / Career
- Money
- Romance
- Family
- Friends
- Home
- Fun and Leisure
- Health and Well-being
- Personal Growth (Spirituality / Education)
- Gifting Time and/or Money (Making a Difference / Community)

Is there a gap between what you say you want and what's actually showing up?

Knowing your values is a powerful way to uncover where there's a disconnect. It's the key to making wise choices in every area of your life, to support your vision and goals. Confusion occurs when you don't take the time to uncover who you are and what you stand for. When you do take the time, and then make choices and take actions in alignment with those values, the outcome is very different.

Here is a list of values to give you some examples.

Integrity	Truth	Fun
Joy	Self-Expression	Spirit
Peace	Justice	Dignity
Leadership	Trust	Discovery

Self-Worth	Humor	Compassion
Honesty	Self-Respect	Perseverance
Loyalty	Spirituality	Respect
Honor	Challenge	Abundance
Prayer	Laughter	Gratitude
Personal Growth	Learning	Harmony
Simplicity	Adventure	Beauty
Calm	Love	Change
Service	Openness	Freedom
Excellence	Community	Goodness
Friendship	Tolerance	Family
Wisdom	Equality	Unity
Courage	Dedication	Kindness

Notice which values stand out and resonate for you. Use this list and add to it as you do the following exercises, to remind you of those important moments in your life.

Action Steps:

Action Step One:

Let's clarify what matters most to you.

- Make a list of ten things you love to do.

  If time and money weren't an issue, if there were no constraints whatsoever, what would you absolutely love to do? Give yourself permission to dream, be outrageous, and have fun with this. If no one were looking or judging, what is it that you would love to do? Write out your list.

1. _____

2. _____

3. _____

4. _____

5. _____

6. _____

7. _____

8. _____

9. _____

10. _____

- What are the three greatest accomplishments in your life so far? What are the three events or moments in your life that have the most significance for you? As you look back over your life, which three moments most amaze you? Which ones make you go "wow" about yourself? Write them down.

LIVE YOUR VALUES

1. _____

   _____

2. _____

   _____

3. _____

   _____

- What are the three most significant events or moments in your life that made you angry, outraged, upset, appalled, etc.? Think back to those moments that caused the biggest reaction. What were they? Write them down.

1. _____

   _____

2. _____

   _____

3. _____

   _____

Action Step Two:

This next step is to deepen your understanding.

- Take the list of the ten things you love to do. For each one write down your answers to the following:

  ♦ What is it about each thing that you "love to do" that you actually love?

  1. _____

  2. _____

  3. _____

  4. _____

  5. _____

  6. _____

  7. _____

  8. _____

  9. _____

  10. _____

LIVE YOUR VALUES

♦ What gives them value to you?

1. _____

2. _____

3. _____

4. _____

5. _____

6. _____

7. _____

8. _____

9. _____

10. _____

♦ What stands out for you as important about each one?

1. _____

2. _____

3. _____

4. _____

5. _____

6. _____

7. _____

8. _____

9. _____

10. _____

- Take the list of your three greatest accomplishments in your life. For each one write your answers to the following:

  ♦ What makes you proudest about each one?

  1. _____

     _____

  2. _____

     _____

  3. _____

     _____

LIVE YOUR VALUES

♦ What makes you go "WOW!" about these events or moments?

1. _____

_____

2. _____

_____

3. _____

_____

♦ What stands out for you as the reason you chose these events or moments as your greatest accomplishments in life?

1. _____

_____

2. _____

_____

3. _____

_____

● Take the list of your most significant events or moments in your life that made you angry, outraged, upset, appalled, etc. For each one write your answers to the following:

♦ What upset you, made you angry or outraged, or appalled you about each of these events or moments?

1. _____

   _____

2. _____

   _____

3. _____

   _____

♦ What wasn't okay with you about each of these events or moments?

1. _____

   _____

2. _____

   _____

3. _____

   _____

♦ What stands out for you as the most outrageous aspect about each of these events or moments?

1. _____

   _____

2. _____

   _____

3. _____

   _____

Action Step Three:

● Now review your answers. "Underneath" each of them is where your values are to be found. Here are some examples:

   ♦ Of the things you love to do:

   If what you love to do is to volunteer at your local homeless shelter, then clearly contribution, service, and making a difference are strong values for you.

   ♦ Of your greatest accomplishments:

   If you chose the birth of your first child, then family and love are very likely important values to you.

   ♦ Of the things that made you angry, etc.:

If your boss, as a regular practice, cuts corners, making you crazy and regularly causing you immense upset, then clearly integrity and honesty are among your core values.

- Go back, look at your answers and think about your values "underneath" your answers.

Action Step Four:

- Make a list of the values that you found by reviewing your answers.

_____	_____
_____	_____
_____	_____
_____	_____
_____	_____
_____	_____
_____	_____
_____	_____

- Pick your top ten values, numbering them from 1-10, one being the most important, and prioritize them.

LIVE YOUR VALUES

1. _____

2. _____

3. _____

4. _____

5. _____

6. _____

7. _____

8. _____

9. _____

10. _____

- Observe your process. Are you making it complicated?
  Is it hard for you to pick and choose? Does this show
  up anywhere else in your life? Write it down.

_____

_____

_____

_____

_____

_____

_____

_____

_____

_____

• Now look at your whole list of ten values and choose three that really resonate with you. Trust yourself. You'll know it when you pick them. You'll hear yourself saying, "Oh, yes, that's me." These are your top three core values.

1. _____

_____

2. _____

_____

3. _____

_____

- NOTE: For those perfectionists among us, yes, you can come back and tweak your list, add to it, and change it!

Now, how are you going to keep your top three values alive in your life? Here are some suggestions:

- Write them on sticky notes, then display them on your monitor, refrigerator, bathroom mirror, dashboard in your car—wherever is prominent for you.

- Keep them on your nightstand so you keep them near in your sleep.

- Put them at the top of each page in your calendar.

- Put them in your tickler/reminder system.

- Set them up as an e-mail to send to yourself every morning.

- Record them: put them on a CD or on your iPod, and play them to yourself throughout the day.

- Make them your screensaver.

BRINGING YOUR VALUES TO LIFE EVERY DAY

Find ways to bring your values to life every day.

If you picked "simplicity," look for ways to simplify your project, your work, and your relationships—in other words, in any and every area of your life.

If family stood out for you as one of your core values, in what ways could you be living that value even more? Are there members of your family you could get closer to or bring together more? What could you do to have your workplace be more like a family?

If you chose "leadership," how and where could you be showing more leadership? What will it take for you to become the leader you want to be starting right now?

If love spoke loudly to you, how could you be more loving? And with whom? How could you bring more love to the world?

Be mindful of your values as you move through your life making decisions and choices, and allow yourself to be guided and inspired by them.

9

KNOW YOUR PURPOSE

"The purpose of life is a life of purpose."

—Robert Byrne

For your vision to truly come alive, it's essential to clarify your purpose. For what reason(s) does your vision excite you? What will accomplishing it bring to your life or the lives of others? For example:

- To be recognized/famous
- To make a difference
- To be happy/fulfilled/proud of yourself
- To be a great mother/father/brother/sister/uncle/aunt/ boss/team member, etc.
- To break a new record
- To have financial freedom
- To have a happy spouse/family/home
- To be secure
- To be kind

- To be authentic
- To be charitable
- To be giving and generous
- To be fully self-expressed
- To cause transformation
- To leave a legacy

When your purpose is at the core of and surrounds everything that you're doing and creating in your life, when you're living it in every area of your **Life Balance Puzzle**, that indeed will be a great life. You'll leap out of bed each morning excited for the day. Nothing will feel like work. And you will truly love your life.

To create a balanced and fulfilled life, your purpose needs to connect to each area of your **Life Balance Puzzle**. Think about how you go about starting a jigsaw puzzle. Usually you sort the pieces into a minimum of two stacks: the inside pieces and the outside "edge" pieces. The next step will be to put the outside "edge" pieces together, to build the border first, which serves as the foundation for successfully filling in the jigsaw puzzle and completing it. In the same way, your life purpose serves as the foundation to living a meaningful, happy, and fulfilled life.

If you look back at how you rated each area in your **Life Balance Puzzle**, you'll probably notice that you're more strongly connected to your life purpose in the areas that you rated the highest. In other words, when the number is low, there's something missing. What are those missing puzzle pieces?

Your life purpose also usually connects with and reflects your core values. Look back over the list of values that you identified as yours. You'll know when you're onto your life purpose because you'll feel excited and free when you express it. And remember to give yourself permission to be excited by your own life purpose. There's nothing like it to energize your life!

An additional powerful benefit when you're in touch with your life purpose is that your mind chatter will decrease. The noise going on in your head will decrease as your life purpose gives you access to that serene core, where you're truly in touch with yourself and what is most important to you.

Your life purpose can evolve, but it doesn't evolve every five minutes. Perfectionists, for example, will want to keep tweaking and changing it. Resist the impulse. Give yourself the experience of accessing something truly powerful and staying with it for a while.

It is your life purpose that will sustain you through doing whatever it takes to accomplish your vision and goals. Think of people you know who are absolutely clear about what they're up to and what they're doing it for—how purposeful and unstoppable, as well as impressive, they are. You're about to become just like them and be the one who dazzles everyone around you, by knowing your purpose and living from it.

Action Steps:

Let's go through some questions to help you clarify your purpose.

- What's the first phrase that comes to mind when you think about what your purpose is? Write it down.

- Note: Just write down the first answer that calls to you. It's okay to write down anything.

_____

_____

_____

_____

_____

- Take it several layers deeper. Keep asking:

  Fill in your answers now to the following questions. It's also a good idea to keep coming back to these questions and expand, refine, even change your answers. As you grow, so will your answers grow.

  ♦ What does this mean for me?

  _____

  _____

KNOW YOUR PURPOSE

_____

_____

_____

♦   What am I here on the planet for?

_____

_____

_____

_____

_____

♦   How does this purpose connect with my values?

_____

_____

_____

_____

_____

♦ What's most important to me?

_____

_____

_____

_____

_____

♦ What truly inspires me?

_____

_____

_____

_____

_____

● Now declare your purpose.

    ♦ Write it as a statement:

My purpose is to _____

_____

_____

KNOW YOUR PURPOSE

_____

_____

_____

_____

_____

_____

Remember, this truly is a life process. It's possible that you may land on something that powerfully resonates for you—it may be your life purpose.

Or you may come back to it, review the questions, refine it, expand it, or even express your purpose differently. And that's okay too.

Your process is your process. Take your time, savor it, and honor it.

10

DESIGN YOUR ROAD MAP

"I find it fascinating that most people plan their vacation with better care than they do their lives. Perhaps that is because escape is easier than change."

—Jim Rohn

So now let's take your vision and transform it into your road map, also known as your action plan—in other words, your outline of what it takes to get there.

CREATE YOUR MILESTONES

In order to create your action plan, the first step is to decide within what period of time you will achieve your overall vision (see Chapter 7). As Stephen Covey says, "Begin with the end in mind." So is it in the next six months? Is it in one year? Or in three or five years?

For example, let's say that your vision is to let go of thirty pounds and to be vibrantly healthy. Most of us don't lose thirty pounds in one week. However, with sustained focus and commitment, it's entirely achievable in, say, six months.

Starting at that end date, write it in the present tense as if it's accomplished:

"I weigh _____ lbs (your current weight less 30 lbs) by _____ (date).

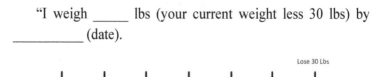

Now you have your timeline from that vision place when your goal is accomplished back to now. Put it in your calendar.

Your timeline from now to your end date is six months, which looks like this:

Starting at your end date and working backwards, create a key milestone. This is a measurable accomplishment on a specific date. For example, at the halfway mark where do you want to be? Let's say half way, which means 15 lbs, as follows:

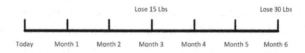

Now decide at what intervals to set additional milestones. If it's monthly and you're focusing on letting go of those thirty pounds, write what you will weigh by the end of six months, then working backwards, what you will weigh by the end of month five, month four, month three, month two, and month one. Using easy math, it looks like this:

DESIGN YOUR ROAD MAP

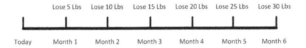

Now chunking it down further, using month one as an example, fill in what you'll weigh at the end of each week. That way you'll be able to track your progress and celebrate your success along the way.

As you plug in these milestones along the timeline, picking specific dates from your end date back to now, showing what will happen by when, this becomes the core of your action plan.

Put the milestones in your calendar—write them in the present tense as if they're done and accomplished.

Important tip: if you're using a paper calendar, write each line item in ink. This is all about commitment and believing in yourself, so no pencil!

Action Steps:

- Decide "by when" you will have achieved your vision. Write down the date.

- Create a list of milestones with specific dates, working backwards from completion to now.

Milestone	Date
_____	_____
_____	_____
_____	_____
_____	_____
_____	_____
_____	_____
_____	_____
_____	_____

- Put your milestones in your calendar.

CREATE YOUR GOALS

Now that you have your key milestones, it's time to flesh out your action plan and create your goals. To do this, quite simply clarify what it will take to accomplish each milestone along the way.

For example, using the same example of losing thirty pounds:

- What specific changes will it take for you to lose the weight?

- What will you be doing less or more of (eating less, drinking more water, exercising more, etc.)? Again, the more specific you are, the easier and quicker it will be to accomplish the goal.

- What support structure will you create for yourself (hire a trainer, walk with a friend on a regular basis, etc.)?

Allow yourself to be messy. Throw everything down, unedited, on paper. Free your mind by getting it all down on paper. Capture every idea that will support you in accomplishing each milestone. Don't worry about perfecting or organizing the list right now—be excited and creative!

Resist the urge to prioritize as you go along, to protect yourself from overcomplicating and paralyzing yourself.

And just a reminder: it's really okay to enjoy this process— in fact, just like creating your vision, it's a great idea to give yourself permission to be excited. If you find yourself getting really significant about your list or anguishing over where to put things, notice it and let it go. Whose list is it? Yours, of course! So you can always move things around and tweak it later. Remember, freedom and ease are the name of the game.

Write these down under each key milestone, chunking them down into achievable, manageable pieces. These pieces are your goals and their "job" is to keep you clear, focused and motivated to reach your milestones. As Mark Victor Hansen says, "Goals are new, forward-moving objectives. They magnetize you toward them."

Now write down what it will take to accomplish each goal— these are your action steps. This sets the process in motion and is the catalyst for the next action and the next action and so on. It clarifies what's next while simplifying and crystallizing your thoughts. Write everything down, prioritize, then chunk them down into achievable, manageable steps (in other words, what it takes step by step to accomplish the goal), then take action.

Now let's prioritize your list of goals and action steps, the most important or urgent items at the top down to the least important or least urgent at the bottom. This is where you'll be making executive decisions about your own action plan, goals, and action steps. You get to say what has the highest priority. Clarify in what order it makes sense to tackle the tasks. Enter them into the action plan with a timeline against each one and simply follow it.

Keep it simple. Resist any urge you may have to complicate things.

NOTES ABOUT GOALS

Write your goals down in the present tense, as if you're already there, and in the positive, because you manifest what you envision.

You may be able to clearly identify what it is you don't want and then wonder why you keep experiencing exactly that! Write down only what it is you *do* want.

Aim high, yet make sure your goals are achievable when you're setting them. And make them exciting. Cause yourself to stretch to keep from being quickly bored by or giving up on your goals. You get to create your own experience here. So what do you choose? How about fun and challenging? To quote Brian Tracy, "Goals in writing are dreams with deadlines."

For now, you're choosing one specific area of your vision to focus on. Later, you can go through this same process and create your vision, action plan, goals, and action steps in every area of your **Life Balance Puzzle**. Ultimately, the pathway to experience balance and fulfillment is to be clear and purposeful, and create powerfully in each area of your life.

Make sure that you really want your goals. It's going to take effort to accomplish them, including: focus, commitment, patience, passion, and perseverance.

Determine whether any of your goals contradict another. It's important that your goals are aligned and not pulling you in multiple directions. With careful planning and vigilance, you can successfully focus on several goals at the same time.

It's important to prioritize both your tasks and your time. This is an important step. Being busy "doing" doesn't necessarily lead to accomplishing your goals. This means clarifying what needs to happen by when to accomplish each goal by the due date.

This is how you will find time for the things you say are important and/or urgent in your life, especially those things you don't like doing. Resist the urge to leave them until last!

In order to experience success along the way, make sure you can accomplish each small action step within the timeline you create for yourself. Adjust it if necessary. It's that simple!

NOTE: Most of us tend to over-schedule ourselves, as well as way underestimate how long each action will take. Allow for contingency time and for life to happen, because it surely will, and take the pressure off.

Remember, it's just a good idea unless it's in your calendar!

Put EVERYTHING—your vision, milestones, goals, and action steps—in your calendar. By doing this, you get to put your stake in the ground and say what's going to happen when, rather than looking back and wondering where your time went. All you then need to do is to stick to your schedule.

Review your goals daily. It can be easy to get off track and to be "slippery" about your goals, especially with yourself. By reviewing your goals daily, you will keep yourself motivated and moving forward, especially if you're excited by your own goals.

Action Steps:

- Create a list of whatever it will take to accomplish each milestone—this is your list of goals.

- Remember, be messy—just capture the ideas.

_____

_____

DESIGN YOUR ROAD MAP

_____

_____

_____

_____

_____

_____

_____

_____

- Now prioritize your list of goals under each milestone.

Milestone: _____   Milestone: _____

Goals: Goals:

_____   _____

_____   _____

_____   _____

_____   _____

_____   _____

IGNITE YOUR LIFE!

_____ _____

_____ _____

_____ _____

_____ _____

Milestone: _____ Milestone: _____

Goals: Goals:

_____ _____

_____ _____

_____ _____

_____ _____

_____ _____

_____ _____

_____ _____

_____ _____

DESIGN YOUR ROAD MAP

- Write down what it will take to accomplish each goal—this is your list of action steps.

Goal: _____   Goal: _____

Action Steps: Action Steps:

_____   _____

_____   _____

_____   _____

_____   _____

_____   _____

_____   _____

_____   _____

_____   _____

Goal: _____   Goal: _____

Action Steps: Action Steps:

_____   _____

_____   _____

_____   _____

_____   _____

_____   _____

_____   _____

_____   _____

- Put EVERYTHING—your vision, milestones, goals, and action steps—in your calendar.

- Review your vision, milestones, goals, and action steps daily to keep yourself motivated and on track.

LIGHTS, CAMERA, ACTION!

"A journey of a thousand miles begins with a simple step."

—Lao-Tzu

You now have your vision in your one chosen area, with key milestones, action plan, goals, and action steps, all with timelines and in your calendar. Congratulations!

Now it's time to get into action!

Take the first step. It's the most important. Once you've taken it, all there is to do is to take the next one and then the next and so on, until the goal is accomplished. The reason for the prior preparation was to get you exactly here—to have it be so clear and so simple, it's a no-brainer. All you have to do is follow your own game plan in your calendar.

Become your own momentum machine. Start now! Don't wait until the time is right, inspiration hits, you have more energy, you feel like it, the stars are aligned, or something outside of yourself and beyond your control is perfect.

Know that momentum comes from within, not without. Waiting for inspiration can be a long wait. Once you begin, the fuel to keep taking the next actions will naturally follow. The more you take action, the more momentum you'll create for yourself.

Stay in action. It's great to have thinking and planning time. However, when you think and plan too much, you go nowhere. Balance all that thinking and planning with action.

Be the person who never gives up. Keep your focus on who you need to be and what you need to do to accomplish the goal. Be willing to do whatever it takes to succeed. Be willing to be courageous, determined, passionate, and focused.

Check your commitment meter. Notice if it's off the charts with bells ringing. Consider what it will take to raise the bar on your resolution and commitment. Ask yourself if you have chosen a powerful goal, one that really lights you up, that you're committed to achieving, and that inspires and motivates you.

If you get off track, get clear what it will take to get back on track—for example, manage distractions, get support, make time—and do so.

The key to success is to keep focusing forwards. Keep moving toward your goal and the fulfillment of your vision.

Track your progress. Measure how you're doing along the way.

Experience and celebrate the successes!

Action Steps:

- What's your first action step? Write it down.

  _____

  Now take action!

- What's your second action step? Write it down.

  _____

  Now go do it!

- What's your third action step? Write it down.

  _____

  Now go get it done!

- What's next...?

  _____

  _____

  _____

  Now keep taking action! Keep the momentum going!

Part Three

LIVE AN
IGNITED LIFE

BE YOUR OWN
BIGGEST CHAMPION

"You are the only person on earth who can use your ability."

—Zig Ziglar

Imagine you're sitting in the bleachers and you're cheering on your favorite player on your team—and, guess what? That favorite player is not only the star of the team, it's also YOU!!!

What would it be like if you supported yourself just like that as you move through your daily life? It would be like your biggest fan following you around all day every day. Could you handle it? Of course you could, but it would take some getting used to; most of us are much more used to noticing what we did wrong, where we screwed up, what we didn't do, and on and on—an endless litany of the negative.

I challenge you to **EMBRACE YOUR MAGNIFICENCE**! There's only one you. That which makes you unique is exclusively yours—own it and embrace it.

And give up comparing and contrasting yourself to others, because each one of us is equally unique. Instead, look for what makes each person unique and embrace that in them.

Be your own biggest champion and notice what shows up!

MANAGE SELF-TALK

Deepak Chopra expresses it so brilliantly: "If you want to reach a state of bliss, then go beyond your ego and the internal dialogue. Make a decision to relinquish the need to control, the need to be approved, and the need to judge. Those are the three things the ego is doing all the time. It's very important to be aware of them every time they come up."

Watch negative self-talk. It can reappear when you're under pressure or confronted by what you're taking on. You might default to beating yourself up and asking yourself disempowering questions. Such as: "Why am I so _____ (stupid, dumb, slow, stubborn, dense, etc.)? Why do I / don't I _____? Why can't I _____?"

Pay attention to the questions you're asking yourself. Be sure they move you forward, inspire you, and motivate you. Otherwise, pick a different question. Major tip: Questions beginning with "why" and "why not" are probably unanswerable and usually put people on the defensive. So avoid asking yourself questions that start with "why," because they will probably stump you at best and paralyze you at worst.

Notice words or phrases that are self-sabotaging. The words *"always"* or *"never"* can make a bad situation worse when it comes to negative self-talk.

BE YOUR OWN BIGGEST CHAMPION

Be aware of how powerful language is, both in thought and spoken word. Sometimes a certain word can have an enormous meaning or charge. For example, when I'm coaching certain clients, if I use the word "*accountability*," it makes them twitch and spasm (when looking for what accountability they are willing to attach to a certain task/action step that they're putting off); however, when I change the word to "*consequence*," it's met with eager acceptance and a quick answer.

Remember that whatever you believe is true. When you believe your goal is possible to achieve and that you will complete it, you will. When you doubt whether it's possible, then you'll drag your heels and sabotage yourself, and that will be true for you. You manifest your belief either way. Take on your goal with gusto and certainty, and you'll amaze yourself at your creativity and resourcefulness.

Be aware of what you're resisting. It's perfectly natural to resist; it's part of the human condition. Change can prompt a "default" to the negative and to resistance.

Push through the mist of your resistance. Embrace that which you really want, and play full out to get it. When using even half the energy you've been using to keep yourself stuck through resistance, you'll be more than halfway there!

Clarify what it will take to overcome your resistance. If it's action that's needed, identify what action it is. If it's acceptance or courage, clarify what it will take. If it's commitment, determine what it will mean on a daily basis, and so on.

Eliminate excuses. Excuses are disempowering. They can protect you in a warm cocoon and stave off having to do anything about them.

Grab your sword and face your excuses head-on. Clarify and list your three main excuses (and make them your best ones!) that will get in the way of achieving your goal. Write down what you will do to overcome each excuse.

Do things now rather than put them off until some vague time in the future. For example, when you think or say, "When I'm (older, taller, thinner, wiser), then I'll _____," or "One day/some day I'll _____," or "Soon I'll _____," this is how you keep it vague and non-specific and merely torture yourself about it.

Ask yourself what you're waiting for. Since none of us actually knows how long we have on this wonderful planet, commit to stop putting things off. *Carpe diem!* Seize the day! Act now!

Say what you mean and mean what you say. Most of us are wonderfully slippery and evasive with our language, giving ourselves lots of wiggle room so that we can't be pinned down. Notice when you're using vague language like "Maybe I'll _____," "I'll try to _____," "I'll probably _____," "It's a possibility that _____," "I'm going to _____," "Sometime I'll _____," and replace it with SPECIFICS.

Watch out for "try." Realize that "trying" to pick up a pen is impossible. You either pick it up or you don't. The pen is an inanimate object and has no feelings, yet we project feelings all over everything, especially when we're resisting or stuck. Notice how often you or others use the word "*try*." Consider how confident you would be about a person's commitment level and capacity for clear accountability and follow-through if he or she regularly "tried" to do the job. Be purposeful in how you express yourself.

Action Steps:

- Be your own biggest champion. Notice what shows up and write it down.

  ♦ For example, maybe it makes you feel uncomfortable, selfish, or egocentric. Maybe you notice people start to help you and it's fun.

  _____

  _____

  _____

  _____

  _____

- Pay attention to negative self-talk. How do you talk to yourself? Be specific. Write it down.

  ♦ For example: I'm not good enough, I'm never going to succeed, I'm way too shy.

_____

_____

_____

_____

- Turn your negative self-talk into positive self-talk.

  ♦ For example: I'm good enough, I achieve success
    with ease, I'm clear and confident.

_____

_____

_____

_____

_____

- When you turn your negative self-talk into positive
  self-talk, what excuses do you come up with to keep
  from doing it?

_____

_____

_____

_____

_____

- What will it take to eliminate your excuses?

_____

_____

_____

_____

_____

- Be focused and committed:

  ♦ Pay attention to how often you use the word "*try.*"
    What could you replace it with? Right now come
    up with 3 active, positive, affirming words you can
    use instead of '*try.*'

    1._____

    2. _____

    3. _____

- What are you putting off? Identify 3 things. For each
  one, write down what it will take to stop putting it off.

  1. _____

2. _____

3. _____

BE YOUR OWN BEST FRIEND

Oprah Winfrey says it so well: "The more you praise and celebrate your life, the more there is in life to celebrate."

Have you ever noticed how hard you are on yourself? In fact, is it true that nobody is harder on you than you yourself?

And how is this working?

Most of us are absolutely brutal with ourselves. We speak to ourselves in ways that we wouldn't speak to anybody else—not even our worst enemies—and certainly nothing like how we speak to our best friends. In a million years, would you ever call your best friend "stupid" or "dummy," no matter what he or she had done? No way! Because that would be the opposite of being a good friend, right? So for what reason would you jump all over yourself (as in beat yourself up) and ask yourself completely disempowering, numbing questions like: "Why am I so stupid?" or "How could I be so dumb?" under ANY circumstances!?

Think of your best friend's voice. How does he or she speak to you? Think of the most loving parent, the most encouraging teacher, the kindest person—surely that is the inner voice that you want to hear?

The most important relationship in your life is your relationship with yourself. The key to building your confidence is to encourage yourself. Become your own best friend and anything will be possible.

Be mindful about how you talk to yourself and how you treat yourself. Are you kind and generous to yourself? Most of us forget ourselves. In the pursuit of success and accomplishment, it's essential that you treat yourself like the superstar that you are.

Be your own best friend. Pay attention to what you think about yourself, how you talk to yourself, what questions you ask yourself, and how you treat yourself. Treat yourself just like you treat your own best friend.

When you make mistakes, how does your best friend react? Is he or she tough and critical? Of course not! Otherwise, you probably wouldn't keep him or her around for too long as your best friend. Give yourself this same gift: learn to forgive yourself and let things go quickly.

Take pride in who you are. This isn't the same as being arrogant. In all humility, embrace what makes you uniquely you—not better or worse than anyone else, just uniquely you—and celebrate everything that you are.

Reward yourself. Review your successes. List your achievements without holding back, without being self-effacing or being stingy with yourself. Celebrate by giving yourself permission to reward yourself.

Action Steps:

- Write down 3 ways you could treat yourself more like your best friend.

  1. _____

  2. _____

  3. _____

- Write down 3 ways you could talk to yourself more like your best friend.

  1. _____

  2. _____

  3. _____

- Write down 3 ways you could reward yourself and celebrate more.

  1. _____

  2. _____

  3. _____

CLEAR THE
MENTAL CLUTTER

"The state of your life is nothing more than a reflection of your state of mind."

—Wayne Dyer

Manage your thoughts. If you were to hear, "Don't think of a pink elephant," what's the first thing you would think about? A lovely plump, pink elephant, of course! Even though you're hearing "don't," the subconscious mind only hears 'a pink elephant.' Your mind will go there even if, and especially when, you're directing it not to. Notice where you're focusing your thoughts.

MIND OVER MATTER

Pay attention to your belief system. Whatever you believe is true. When you believe something is hard or impossible, it is. When you believe it's easy and completely possible, remarkably it shows up that way. The common ingredient is you. Stay alert to your beliefs!

Eliminate your excuses. Take that same energy that you're using to determine every reason why not and focus it on solutions and ways to make your goal happen. Watch out for procrastination. This is surely when your mind is in protection-and-survival mode, giving everything it has to keep you right where you are by bringing up fear, over-thinking, doubt, and every form of negative self-talk to paralyze you. You're greater than any and all of these negative voices in your head. All it takes is to stay alert, not get hooked by them, and thank them for sharing—then keep moving forward.

Is that inner dialogue that you're having with yourself depressing or inspiring? Have you even noticed that you've been engaging in an inner dialogue? It can be insidious and sneak up on you when you're least expecting it. So be aware. Simply notice it when it begins to turn to the negative and adjust it either by reminding yourself about all your progress and accomplishments or by asking yourself an inspiring question—for example, "How shall I celebrate today?" or "What's my next action step to move me even closer toward reaching my goal?"

Dare to reach. Have the courage to reach for your dreams, instead of talking yourself out of them or listening to others' limiting beliefs. Take the first step, which is surely your most important, then the next, and then the next. Take one step at a time—and keep it simple.

Be aware of negative self-talk. Listen to the questions you ask yourself. Change them when they're paralyzing and demotivating (why can't I / don't I / do I?), especially when they include the words "*always*" or "*never*." Pick a question that inspires you and moves you forward, like "What will it take to _____?"

For the perfectionists in our midst, it's especially important to be vigilant with those marvelous voices in your head. How they will keep you in place (in other words, not moving forward) is by having you go over and over the smallest of details, and then over and over them again just in case you might have missed one small dot over one '*i*', and exhaust you into paralysis. From the heart of this recovering perfectionist—yours truly—the way out of this maze is to allow it to be "*good enough*" versus "*perfect*" before taking the next step. Give yourself the gift of completing whatever it is that you're up to. When you're done, you can always go back and review it after you have completed it. On a personal note, imagine how challenging it was for me to allow myself to complete the first draft of this book, and then how many drafts and changes I went through until I allowed it to be complete!

Do something different when you're stuck. Doing the same thing the same way is likely to produce the same result. Ask yourself what you could be doing differently.

Beware of absolutes. When you think in absolutes you define yourself and others with words like "*always*" and "*never*." Let go of judging and defining. Practice removing those words from your thinking and speaking. Notice how freeing it is.

When something goes right, notice it. Then do it again. And remember to celebrate!

Believe in yourself. Let go of worrying about and focusing on what others think of you. Get clear about what you're up to in the world, who you are, what you stand for, and where you want to make a difference. Be true to yourself.

Be that which you want in others. This sounds incredibly simple, and it is. When you want better communication with someone, talk with him or her more often and be more open. Go first when you want more affection. Be more tender and loving. Do it without strings attached, without attachment to the outcome.

Be mindful of who you surround yourself with. Pay attention to how others are reacting to your vision and goals, and to what they're saying. It can be easy to let doubters and naysayers influence you. It can be enlightening and immensely empowering to thank them for sharing their thoughts (usually negative) and ideas (often based on limiting beliefs), and still keep moving forward.

Create a strong support system of mentors, colleagues, friends, and family. Most successful people surround themselves with superstars. Take a look at who you surround yourself with. Invite them to support you in who you are and what you aspire to achieve.

Keep yourself firmly in the present and be on the lookout for creative ideas and solutions to achieve success today. It's so tempting to look back at the past or forward into the future and come up with excuses why things haven't worked out before or will be difficult, if not insurmountable, in the future. Be in the now!

Do it differently. To keep doing things the same way just because that's the way you have always done them is the quickest formula to keep yourself stuck and bored. Be creative. Turn your project upside down. Explore looking at it in different ways. Ask yourself how else you could be thinking about it, designing it, and implementing it.

You owe it to yourself to get and stay excited!

Do what you think you can't do. You'll discover how delicious it is to pull off the impossible.

Action Steps:

- Describe what your most powerful negative self-talk sounds like.

  _____

  _____

  _____

  _____

  _____

- Review your list of top OUCHES and GIGGLES. Write down the top 3 that are keeping you stuck.

  1. _____

  2. _____

3. _____

- Write down 3 actions that you're going to take to overcome them and keep moving forward.

  1. _____

  2. _____

  3. _____

- What negative self-talk and excuses are coming up right now to derail you from taking action?

  ♦ List three main excuses that get in the way of achieving your goal. For each one write down what you will do to overcome it.

  ♦ Use the Action Steps from Chapter 12 to change the negative self-talk.

  1. _____

  2. _____

  3. _____

CHOOSE POWERFULLY

To quote Groucho Marx: *"Every morning when I open my eyes I say to myself: I, not the events, have the power to make me happy or unhappy today. I can choose which it will be. Yesterday is dead, tomorrow hasn't arrived yet. I have just one day, today, and I'm going to be happy in it."*

Remember, you always have choices. You always do, especially when you think you don't!

The way out of a stuck place is to clarify what choices you have rather than buying into the belief that you don't have any choices.

Take time making your choices and picking your goals. Then choose clearly and powerfully. The alternative is self-torture and regret, both of which are an energy drain and a huge waste of time.

Make a list of all the choices you discover, no matter how small or "silly" you think they are. Pick one and take an action on that choice, then another, and so on. Before long, you will see how full of choices every moment of your life truly is.

Let go of self-doubt. Think about how precious time and energy are, and how much you are wasting on second-guessing yourself. Then soar with the eagles!

Realize that you get to choose what you have/do/be in your life and also how you experience it along the way. Pay attention to what is working and what isn't working. And make some new choices…

Be at peace with your choices. It's impossible to find peace of mind when you hesitate, vacillate, repeatedly change your mind, and worry about the choices you made, what other people think, and the infinite "what ifs" that you may manufacture. All the frustrations disappear when you're at peace with the choices you make. Commit and stick to your choices once you choose. Watch most of your frustrations evaporate.

Choose your experience. You get to choose what you have in your life, what to add to it, what you take on and do, and how you experience it. You get to choose not only what you're doing, but also how you experience it.

Notice that you can choose your reaction to what shows up in your life. Look at yourself in your relationship with a loved one, child, friend, boss, or colleague. Look at your part of the equation in that relationship. Think about how you could be reacting differently to produce a different result than, say, frustration. Choose rather than react.

Know that where you choose to focus will determine your experience. Stop beating yourself up for having "failed." Rather, seek out opportunities to learn, to become clear about what you won't repeat, to know what to do differently, and to add to your treasure chest of insights. There's no such thing as failure! It's all about the lessons learned.

Create rather than react. Today is the day to be the pioneer of your future. If you choose, so is tomorrow, and the next day, and the next. Living and creating this way, you will surely become fearless, courageous, and unstoppable!

Action Steps:

- If you knew that you couldn't fail, right now what would you choose to do? Write it down.

_____

_____

_____

_____

- How would you choose to experience whatever you just chose? Write it down.

_____

_____

_____

_____

_____

- Write down 3 actions that you're going to take to bring it alive?

    1. _____

    2. _____

    3. _____

MASTER YOUR TIME

"Time is our most valuable asset, yet we tend to waste it, kill it, and spend it rather than invest it."

—Jim Rohn

Most of us are overloaded with places to get to, meetings to have, things to do, calls to make or return, e-mails to read or reply to, projects to complete, and people to see or talk to or take care of. Many of us flail around like wet fish, reacting to whatever shouts the loudest with the greatest level of urgency, and manage to make it through another day.

So where does all the time go?

SHIFT YOUR RELATIONSHIP TO TIME

As Charles Bruxton says so well, "You will never 'find' time for anything. If you want time, you must make it."

What if there's another way to experience this thing called time? What if it were possible to be at the helm of your ship, guiding it through calmer waters versus bouncing around, reacting all day long? This invites the inquiry: what would it take to master time?

It starts with giving up all your excuses about not having enough time and getting clear about what's most important or urgent in your life.

Make the time. There's no such thing as being too busy or not having enough time. When something is important enough to you, you magically "find" the time.

Make your project important and urgent, declare it so, and watch how you have enough time for that and everything else.

An example that I use with clients who are struggling with "finding the time" is to ask them: If they had the life-saving serum that I needed to save my life and I needed it by 5:00 p.m. that same day, would I be able to count on them to get it to me on or preferably before that time? Without exception, each has readily replied, "Absolutely. You can count on me." I'm infinitely grateful each time I hear their earnest concern and commitment to keeping me alive. And I challenge them to take a look at their level of focus and commitment to the accomplishment of their goal, as well as the level of urgency that they're attributing to it—and to raise the bar.

Action Steps:

- Where are you lacking enough time in your life right now?

_____

_____

_____

_____

- What are your reasons and excuses?

_____

_____

_____

_____

_____

- How can you make that more important and urgent?

_____

_____

_____

_____

_____

- What difference does that make?

_____

_____

_____

_____

_____

SCHEDULE PLANNING TIME

Richard Eyre powerfully suggests, "Don't just do something, sit there! Sit there long enough each morning to decide what is really important during the day ahead."

It's essential to resist the urge to hit the ground running, leaping into action to deal with whatever is screaming the loudest to be taken care of. Give yourself the gift of thinking, planning, and prioritizing time for fifteen to thirty minutes at the beginning of each day. If you prefer to do this at the end of the day, do so. However, my recommendation is to start the day this way, to create and design your day.

And once a week, preferably on the weekend, give yourself thirty minutes to take stock of the previous week's accomplishments and celebrate them. Then plan for the week ahead. You'll be amazed at the results, especially in the areas of purposefulness, focus, productivity, effectiveness, energy, accomplishment, and enjoying life.

Remember to calendar everything. If you don't, when will you have the time? At the end of the day, do you ever wonder where all the time went and wonder what on earth you actually got done? This comes from not scheduling and not knowing what you're doing and when. When you calendar everything, all you'll need to do is keep to the schedule that you create for yourself. If you notice that you don't have enough time even after having scheduled, take a look at whether you're underestimating how long things take and allow more time.

Stick to your schedule. If something comes up and you have to move something - perhaps you have a conflict or you've overscheduled yourself - find another time and re-schedule it. The mistake most of us make, especially when it has to do with ourselves, is we give everything else priority and just let what's most important to us either slide or evaporate completely, instead of treating it like a million-dollar meeting and re-scheduling it. This especially applies to exercise!

If you don't already have one, pick a scheduling system. Let go of relying on your memory. Relieve the pressure on yourself by creating somewhere to put everything.

Prioritize your time. Put absolutely *everything* into your schedule, because everything takes time. Schedule everything so you can accurately map out your time.

Another important reason to calendar everything is: when you know when you're going to do something, it greatly increases the odds you'll actually do it.

Especially pay attention to scheduling appointments with yourself. That includes exercise, meals, breaks, and those activities you expect to do later. This will minimize the impact of "life happening" (which we can count on) and things getting in the way.

Move beyond assuming that you'll find the time for your less favorite tasks. Schedule some time for administrative tasks, like returning calls and replying to e-mails. As you develop the habit of putting everything into your calendar, you'll have more control over your day. Less and less chaos will show up, and you'll accomplish more.

Action Steps:

- Calendar fifteen to thirty minutes at the beginning of each day to plan the day.

- Calendar thirty minutes once a week, preferably on the weekend, to review the previous week's accomplishments, celebrate them, and plan for the week ahead.

- Calendar everything, especially and including appointments with yourself.

- What happens when you keep to your schedule? Write it down.

MASTER YOUR TIME

_____

_____

_____

GET ORGANIZED

"It's hard to be fully creative without structure and constraint. Try to paint without a canvas. Creativity and freedom are two sides of the same coin. I like the best of both worlds. Want freedom? Get organized. Want to get organized? Get creative."

—David Allen

Getting organized starts with having a system. So let's take a look at the key elements of an easy system to manage.

Remember to create a master to-do list. Include **EVERYTHING**, no matter how small. Resist the temptation to leave out the small stuff, thinking, *"I'll just take care of that right now. It'll only take a minute."* It probably won't.

Name your to-do list something that lights you up, that makes you smile, something you actually want to look at. The goal is to use it and use it often. Give yourself permission to have fun with naming it. For example, mine is called, "Andrea's Great Adventure!" Some other ideas might be: "Vision Quest," "My Multi-Million-Dollar Treasure Chest"—anything that lights you up and has you eager to use it!

Add a "by when" to as many items as possible on your to-do list. That means a date and a time. The more specific, the better. Your to-do's will spring to life. You'll become clearer about what you're doing and when it needs to be done.

Put all of your to-do's with clear timelines into your schedule, whether you hand-write them in your calendar or enter them into your computer and/or PDA. Remember, it's just a good idea if it's not in your schedule.

Clear your desk of clutter. It's hard to think clearly when you are surrounded by "stuff." Why make it hard on yourself? Also, let go of clutter wherever it is in your house—and you'll let go of frustration, chaos, and stress.

For example, create a system to manage the paper. Remember, the secret to any system is that it works for you, so you'll use it regularly. And it's also a great idea to be able to find it again at a later date!

Sort your piles of paper into categories.

For example, a simple system to manage paper is:

- ACTION
- FILE
- READ
- TOSS

Decide how you're going to prioritize your ACTION papers. A simple accordion file with thirty-one slots will provide a simple solution to managing the paper throughout the month. The secret to success with this system is to check the accordion file at the beginning of each day to make sure that you take care of whatever needs your attention that day. And remember to add the action items into your master to-do list, with a clear "by when," and calendar them.

The FILE papers can either be filed immediately if time permits or, if not, can be put into a "TO BE FILED" file. In the latter case, schedule time to take care of the filing. Or even better, seek out help to get it done.

Create a READING file or pile and schedule reading time in your calendar. Remember, everything takes time, so when will you do it if it's not scheduled?

The TOSS pile is clearly to be thrown away. Remember to shred confidential or sensitive papers.

Action Steps:

- Create a master to-do list.
  - ◆ Remember to include EVERYTHING.
  - ◆ Name it something that inspires you and Ignites Your Life!
  - ◆ Add a "by when" to every item and calendar everything.
  - ◆ Refer to it and add to it every day.
- Clear the clutter in your office and home. Where do you have clutter? What system will work for you to keep it clear?
  - ◆ Create a system to keep the clutter cleared and use it.

♦ For example, e-mail: when you will read it (e.g. 2 x a day), what you will do with it (make a decision, act on it, save it in a folder, delete it).

_____

_____

_____

_____

_____

NOTE: Keep it simple. Create what you'll actually use.

16

CHOOSE EASY VS. HARD

"Do not let what you cannot do interfere with what you can do."

—John Wooden

Imagine that I'm standing in front of you right now, with both of my hands outstretched toward you with palms up to heaven. I point to my right hand—this represents "EASY." I point to my left hand—this represents "HARD." Now think about the area you've been focusing on in your life from the **Life Balance Puzzle**. If you could choose for that to be easy or hard, what would you choose?

It seems like an obvious answer, doesn't it? Did you choose "EASY"? Excellent! In fact, throughout my entire numerous years of coaching, not one person has ever chosen "hard" on any topic! However, without someone outside ourselves asking such a simple question, most of us naturally and unconsciously default to choosing "hard," even though we would fiercely deny it. Have you ever noticed that you weren't necessarily choosing the easiest path to get to where you wanted to go in life?

It's all in the questions you ask yourself. Pay attention to the questions you ask yourself and notice firstly if they're serving you, and secondly how you answer.

And know that you always have choice, especially when you think you don't.

So think about the area you're focusing on. If you could choose for it to be easy, what would it look like?

Allow others to help you. There's no rule that says you have to do everything yourself. There's all kinds of help all around you for the asking. Get clear about what it is you need, then reach out and ask for it. The worst that can happen is someone will say no. There's nothing to lose by asking. And most people are just waiting to be asked. Have you noticed how often people actually want to help when you just ask?

Let go of being significant. Give yourself permission to lighten up. It's okay to laugh and to be amused by yourself and life in order to access your creative side.

Remove whatever is unnecessary. Take an inventory of what you could let go of or give up, on either a temporary or permanent basis, to accomplish your goals.

Make your goal important. Treat your goal as if you need to be at a certain place at a certain time to get a life-saving serum. You would probably be there, and early, correct?! Elevate the level of urgency and the results will be extraordinary.

Be like a laser beam. Laser beams are dazzling and direct. Be powerfully intentional in your life. The more you say how it will go, the quicker it will show up exactly that way.

Identify what roadblocks and challenges are appearing along the way. Consider what's stopping you from accomplishing your goal. Create a list. Your roadblocks could be primarily yourself, in the form of procrastination, over-thinking, and self-sabotage. The roadblocks might be others, with their opinions and limiting beliefs about you and/or your goal. Or they might be events that suddenly occur that you hadn't counted on taking up your time.

So how are you helping or hindering your progress?

Be clear about who you will be in the face of challenge, no matter where it arises from. You can choose to be confronted and stopped, or you can choose to be persistent, confident, and courageous.

Action Steps:

- Are you truly choosing easy vs. hard? If not, what would easy look like? How would it be different? If it were easy, what would you be doing differently?

_____

_____

_____

_____

_____

- Who do you choose to be to accomplish your goals? How do you become that person?

  _____

  _____

  _____

  _____

  _____

♦ What kind of help do you need?

  _____

  _____

  _____

  _____

♦ Who do you know who can provide that help?

  _____

  _____

  _____

_____

_____

◆   When will you ask them for help?

_____

_____

_____

_____

_____

●   Remember to choose "EASY"? Create reminders to make it easy and keep you on track (calendar, sticky notes, string on the wrist, support team, etc.).

17

TAKE CARE OF YOURSELF

"Only by feeling compassion for yourself can you feel compassion for others. If you cannot love yourself, you cannot love others and you cannot stand to see others loved. If you cannot treat yourself kindly, you will resent that treatment when you see it in anyone else."

—Gary Zukav

Take a look at where you're prioritizing yourself in your already busy life, if at all. Most of us good, decent people tend to do a really great job of taking care of our immediate circle, our close family and friends, and our work team, maybe extending to include our community. Most people I've coached over the years forget to give themselves even minor supporting roles in the movies called their lives, let alone starring roles!

Put yourself first. It's essential to some degree to put yourself first in order to focus, achieve, and accomplish. That doesn't mean be selfish and absolutely disregard everyone and everything. What it does mean is to get clear, create a plan for yourself, then communicate it clearly to those who will be involved and impacted and enroll their support. Ironically, in order to have the reserve to be there for everyone in your life, it's essential to put yourself first.

Get enough rest. Look into what's waking you up if you're not sleeping through the night. Keep a worry pad next to your bed to jot down your worries. Let them go until the next day and give yourself permission to sleep. Discover any other reasons you're waking up and seek solutions.

Take breaks during the day. Take a lunch break, both to nourish yourself and to clear your head, as well as to renew your perspective. Take short breaks, especially when you feel paralyzed, unclear, or overwhelmed. Step away from your desk. Go for a walk around the block. Talk to a colleague. Do something to refresh yourself and re-balance.

Get regular exercise. Moving your body energizes you, clears your mind, and supports achieving outstanding results.

Notice what you're eating and drinking, and whether you're choosing wisely. Nourish your body with healthy food and lots of water. Stay conscious about what your body needs in order to be energized and to operate at optimum levels. Learn what those food choices are if you don't know.

Action Steps:

- Write down 3 ways to put yourself first more in your life.

    1. _____

    2. _____

    3. _____

- Change your schedule to make sure you get enough rest. What 3 changes can you make right now?

    1. _____

    2. _____

    3. _____

- Take breaks throughout the day and notice what's different. Write it down.

    _____

    _____

    _____

    _____

    _____

- How often are you exercising? Write down 3 ways to increase your level of activity.

  ♦ For example, walk up a flight of stairs instead of using the elevator.

  1. _____

  2. _____

  3. _____

- How are you feeding your body? How can you improve on this?

  ♦ For example, eat less pre-packaged food and more fresh fruit and vegetables.

  _____

  _____

  _____

  _____

  _____

- How are you feeding your soul? What can you be doing to nurture your spirit?
  - ◆ For example, read inspiring books and listen to uplifting music.

_____

_____

_____

_____

_____

18

EXPERIENCE GRATITUDE

"Gratitude unlocks the fullness of life. It turns what we have into enough, and more. It turns denial into acceptance, chaos into order, confusion into clarity...It turns problems into gifts, failures into success, the unexpected into perfect timing, and mistakes into important events. Gratitude makes sense of our past, brings peace for today and creates a vision for tomorrow."

—Melodie Beattie

The most powerful place to start anything is right where you are. So let's begin by taking an inventory of everything you're grateful for right now in your life. The more you do this, the more you'll become aware of what you're overlooking, what you're taking for granted. This might include:

- Your health
- Your spouse
- Your children
- Your parents
- Your siblings
- Your pets

- Your home
- Your garden
- Your friends
- Good food
- Your vacation
- Your business or job
- Your colleagues
- The blue sky
- A tree

Whatever you focus on expands. Be an attractor magnet. According to the Law of Attraction, as you develop the muscle called "Gratitude" and you focus on all the blessings in your life, you become the magnet for attracting more and more blessings. So every day give thanks.

The place of gratitude is one of acceptance and appreciation.

Be grateful for everything, including the challenges. After all, it's all in how you frame them. Most often our obstacles and challenges in life turn out to be our greatest lessons and our greatest opportunities for growth—for seeing what we're truly capable of overcoming and achieving, and for feeling proud of ourselves.

When things "go wrong," seek out the greater good, and your and others' higher good. Look for what else there might be in the situation to be grateful for—and give thanks.

Create a focused moment every day to focus on gratitude. An excellent way of grounding this is to use a Gratitude

Journal—go to the following link to learn more: **www.IgniteYourLifeBook.com.**

It's a great way to start the day. Take five minutes first thing in the morning and write down five things you're truly grateful for: your health, the sunshine, your warm comfortable bed—whatever comes to mind.

Do this as a daily practice. Start the day this way and notice how it changes your day. As you write in your journal day by day, notice what changes begin to show up in your life. Anthony Robbins reminds us: "When you are grateful fear disappears and abundance appears."

Remember to draw from every area of your life—whatever you're feeling grateful for that day.

As you do this more and more, notice how your awareness expands. Start to notice the small moments and "see" the precious opportunities that are simple yet beautiful, fleeting yet most meaningful.

Let your heart awaken to the transforming power of gratitude.

Action Steps:

- What are you grateful for right now in your life? Take an inventory and give yourself permission to truly feel gratitude as you write it all down.

_____

_____

_____

- Begin every morning by taking five minutes to write
  five things you're grateful for in your Gratitude
  Journal.

- Notice what happens and how it affects your day. Write
  it down.

_____

_____

_____

_____

_____

- As you do this day after day, what changes are you
  noticing showing up in your life? Write it down.

_____

_____

_____

EXPERIENCE GRATITUDE

ENJOY THE JOURNEY

"Now is the only time there is. Make your now wow, your minutes miracles, and your days pay. Your life will have been magnificently lived and invested, and when you die you will have made a difference."

—Mark Victor Hansen

It's important and great to have a vision, with goals, an action plan, milestones, and action steps. However, if you're only focusing on the destination, you're missing out on the experience—namely the journey. Most of our greatest moments, experiences, and lessons happen along the way, rather than at the moment of accomplishment and completion. You get to create your own experience and you get to choose. Which will it be? Here are some tips to guide you along the way:

Enjoy the journey.

It's all a process. Be okay with it.

Honor the process.

Make sure you're not rushing toward the finish line with only the goal in mind. Enjoy the process. By giving yourself permission to have fun, to play, and to celebrate, the results usually far exceed your expectations, and you'll have a great time along the way.

Have patience rather than demanding instant gratification, wanting it now, killing yourself to get it, or destroying relationships, exhausting yourself, letting your health suffer, and so on.

Give yourself permission to experience and live a balanced life, even if and especially when you're striving in one or more areas of your life. You can "have it all." It's all in how you design it. Use your **Life Balance Puzzle**—keep checking in with how you feel about every area of your life and how they're all working together.

Celebrate the special moments and the successes along the way. It's all too easy to experience life like a hamster being experimented on, running round and round that wheel, rushing from one task to the next. Pause and celebrate your small achievements and successes along the way to keep yourself energized and enjoying the journey.

Accomplishment is great—contentment, balance, and fulfillment are even greater.

Life happens in the small moments along the way.

Savor the moments.

Remember to stay true to yourself and to live in alignment with your values.

Go slowly enough so that you can see the opportunities and learn the lessons along the way.

Smell the roses as you journey through this wonderful adventure called your life.

Action Steps:

- Remember to enjoy the journey!
- Enjoy more happiness, fulfillment, and success day by day… as you Ignite Your Life!

DISCOVER THE SECRETS TO LIVING THE LIFE YOU LOVE

Go here now to claim your *free* gift immediately!

www.IgniteYourLifeGift.com

Congratulations! Now that you have begun the journey to Igniting Your Life, it's time to bring it alive on a whole new level.

Go to **www.IgniteYourLifeGift.com** immediately to claim your free gift:

"The 7 Secrets to Living the Life You Love"

Are you ready to truly *Ignite Your Life*? Well, you've come to the right place because I'm about to guide you so that you'll easily be able to move powerfully toward the life you have been dreaming about. In this 7 part audio series, I will personally help you uncover what has been holding you back, and help you transform your life from one of worry, fear, stress, overwhelm and procrastination into a life filled with passion, purpose and fulfillment.

This 7 part audio series (available as mp3 downloads), along with the transcripts, will inspire and motivate you to take action today and start living the Life You Love!

Please accept this gift with my love and gratitude and best wishes for success in every area of your life.

Go immediately to the link below to *Ignite Your Life* NOW!

www.IgniteYourLifeGift.com

BUY A SHARE OF THE FUTURE IN YOUR COMMUNITY

These certificates make great holiday, graduation and birthday gifts that can be personalized with the recipient's name. The cost of one S.H.A.R.E. or one square foot is $54.17. The personalized certificate is suitable for framing and will state the number of shares purchased and the amount of each share, as well as the recipient's name. The home that you participate in "building" will last for many years and will continue to grow in value.

Here is a sample SHARE certificate:

YES, I WOULD LIKE TO HELP!

I support the work that Habitat for Humanity does and I want to be part of the excitement! As a donor, I will receive periodic updates on your construction activities but, more importantly, I know my gift will help a family in our community realize the dream of homeownership. **I would like to SHARE in your efforts against substandard housing in my community!** *(Please print below)*

PLEASE SEND ME _____ SHARES at $54.17 EACH = $ $_____

In Honor Of: _____

Occasion: (Circle One)   HOLIDAY   BIRTHDAY   ANNIVERSARY

     OTHER: _____

Address of Recipient: _____

Gift From: _____ *Donor Address:* _____

Donor Email: _____

I AM ENCLOSING A CHECK FOR $ $_____ **PAYABLE TO HABITAT FOR**

HUMANITY OR PLEASE CHARGE MY VISA OR MASTERCARD *(CIRCLE ONE)*

Card Number _____ Expiration Date: _____

Name as it appears on Credit Card _____ Charge Amount $ _____

Signature _____

Billing Address _____

Telephone # Day _____ Eve _____

PLEASE NOTE: Your contribution is tax-deductible to the fullest extent allowed by law.
Habitat for Humanity • P.O. Box 1443 • Newport News, VA 23601 • 757-596-5553
www.HelpHabitatforHumanity.org

Printed in the USA
CPSIA information can be obtained
at www.ICGtesting.com
JSHW082209140824
68134JS00014B/520